TABLE OF CONTENTS

Page

TABLE OF CONTENTS.. i

ACRONYMS.. iii

ILLUSTRATIONS iv

CHAPTER ONE INTRODUCTION..1

Background.. 1
Primary Research Question 6
Secondary Research Questions.. 6
Significance 6
Assumptions.. 7
Limitations 8

CHAPTER 2 LITERATURE REVIEW 9

Introduction.. 9
The Terrorist Threat... 10
The Borders, Immigration, and Regional Terrorism 12
Border Security 25
US Legislation, Strategy, and Policy 41
Methodology 48

CHAPTER 3 RESEARCH METHODOLOGY 51

Introduction.. 51
Research Design 51

CHAPTER 4 ANALYSIS..54

Introduction.. 54
Terrorist Requirements 54
Myth of the Mexican Menace 58
The Canadian Conundrum... 64

Effects of the Fence 69
US Policy 77

CHAPTER 5 CONCLUSIONS AND RECOMMENDATIONS 82

Conclusions 82
Recommendation 84
Recommendations For Further Research 86
Summary 87

GLOSSARY 89

APPENDIX A TERRORIST IMMIGRATION TABLE 90

REFERENCE LIST 94

ACRONYMS

BEA	Bureau of Economic Analysis
CBO	Congressional Budget Office
CBP	Customs and Border Protection
CGSC	Command General Staff College
CRS	Congressional Research Service
DOD	Department of Defense
DHS	Department of Homeland Security
GAO	Government Accountability Office
OTM	Other Than Mexican
POE	Port of Entry
SBI	Secure Border Initiative
USBP	United States Border Patrol

ILLUSTRATIONS

Page

Figure 1. Proposed Border Fence According to the Secure Fence Act of 2006.................2

Figure 2. Photo of the San Diego Fence...3

Figure 3. Route of GAO Investigators at U.S.-Mexico Border Location 28

Figure 4. Military Organizational Requirements 55

Figure 5. Map of Border Patrol Sectors Along the Southwest Border...........................71

Figure 6. Apprehensions at San Diego Sector Stations and Tucson Sector....................72

Figure 7. US Real GDP for FY1992 through FY2004 and Percentage GDP Growth for
            FY1990 through FY2004...74

CHAPTER ONE

INTRODUCTION

Background

The faces of the nineteen hijackers responsible for the 9/11 attacks on the US will

forever remain branded in the memory of those who lived through those days of crisis.

Calls to remember the murdered victims and pledges to never again allow such an attack

to occur have permeated nearly every act of security legislation and Presidential Directive

following that national disaster. In this current political atmosphere, the measure of a

leader's label of "strong on terrorism" provides the defining credential for political office.

A perceived lack of control over any potential territorial access by a terrorist must be

aggressively corrected to ensure political survival. These same images of terrorists, along

with images of armed border citizens hiding behind residential fortresses in fear of a

terrorist-imbedded immigrant invasion, pervade the news networks and fuel the cry for

defense of the US-Mexico border.

Current immigration policy has become a volatile issue, and has caused great

divergence in the American populace, resulting in proposed immigration reform

legislation in 2005-2006.[1] Although its intent was to reduce the tide of illegal

immigrants, reduce terrorist threat, and reduce social service cost, the bill was not

successful, in part due to opposing movements in both political parties and perceived

constituent opposition (Rasmussen Reports 2007). Perhaps more importantly, nationwide

---

[1] The USHouse of Representatives passed the *Border Protection, Antiterrorism, and Illegal Immigration Control Act of 2005,* HR 4437 on December 16, 2005. The US Senate passed the *Comprehensive Immigration Reform Act of 2006*. S 2611 on May 25, 2006. Neither Bill received enough votes to pass both houses of Congress.

public demonstrations fueled this emotionally-laden issue (Jacobs 2006). In a response to appease the American populace and ensure a political win, the one bill that was successful was the Secure Fence Act of 2006, which mandated the Department of Homeland Security to build 700 plus miles of border fence along the 2,000 mile US-Mexico border (Secure Fence Act 2006, 2) (see figure 1). This congressional action was taken just one month prior to the 2006 US midterm elections.

Border Fencing According to the 2006 Fence Act

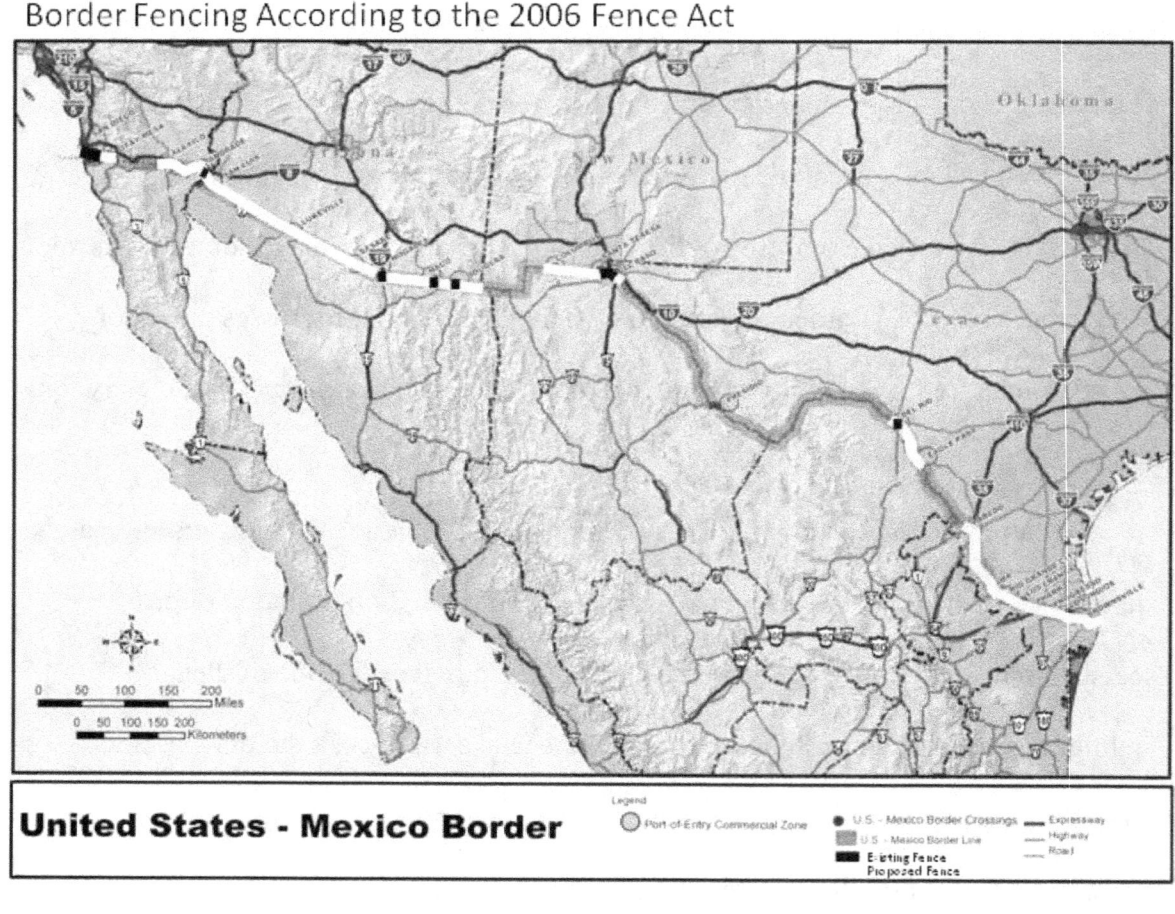

Figure 1. Proposed Border Fence According to the Secure Fence Act of 2006
Source: Public Domain, Author added existing and proposed fencing graphics

In 2006 the President signed into law the Secure Fence Act. This Act mandated the composition be of at least two layers of reinforced fencing along specific geographical points with deadlines for initiation and completion of different portions of the project. The legislative description of the design of the border fence suggests a modeling based upon the previously constructed San Diego fence (see figure 2). The Act did not provide funding for the border fence, however, suggesting that this was more of a politically-motivated action rather than a real attempt to secure our borders. It is estimated that the construction and maintenance of the fence for a 25 year lifespan will cost $49 billion (Hendricks 2007). The construction of a border fence between the US and Canada has also been proposed, but to date, no congressional legislation has been drafted. The massive costs associated with the land length of 3,145 miles, coupled with the perceived lower immigration impact on this Northern border, may be the underlying reason for congressional inaction.

Figure 2.   Photo of the San Diego Fence
Source: Public Domain

3

On December 26, 2007 the President signed into law the omnibus appropriations bill that in effect removed the specifications requirements in the 2006 Secure Fence Act and provided an initial $1.2 billion toward the construction of border protection fencing, technology, and infrastructure (Consolidated Appropriations Act 2008, 204). The Department of Homeland Security (DHS) is now acting on the construction of only portions of a border fence. This is an attempt not only to control illegal immigration and drug traffic, but also primarily now as another way to ensure the security of the nation from terrorist attack.

Ironically, none of the 9/11 attackers entered the US surreptitiously through our Northern or Southern border. In fact, all of the 9/11 hijackers entered the country on legitimate visas, and only 6 had violated them by over-staying, enrolling in school when they entered as tourists, or failing to enroll when they entered as students. The capture of Palestinian terrorist Gazi Ibrahim Abu Mezer in 1997 and the Algerian terrorist Ahmed Ressam in 1999 provide the only examples of a physical attempt to cross our Northern or Southern border by a terrorist. Abu Mezer made his crossing along the northwest US-Canada border (Egan 1997), and Ressam was apprehended at a Port of Entry (POE) by US customs officers during his attempted crossing (Bernton, Carter, Heath, and Neff 2002, Chapter 12). All other captures of foreign terrorists plotting to carry out terrorist attacks on US soil have taken place outside of US borders.

Although the current movement among the populace to secure our borders via a border fence primarily occurred as a result of the 9/11 attacks in 2001, its initial construction occurred in response to illegal immigration and drug traffic across the US-

Mexico border. The United States Border Patrol (USBP) began erecting barriers near San Diego as a part of their deterrence strategy in 1990. In 1996 the Congressional Illegal Immigration Reform and Immigrant Responsibility Act provided the Attorney General, and now DHS, authority to construct barriers along the border. Completion of this portion of a border fence was stalled due to environmental legal action against its construction. In 2005 Congress passed the REAL ID Act which allowed the Department of Homeland Security to waive all legal requirements to expedite the completion of the San Diego fence. Following the congressional action, DHS stated that it intends to use these powers to complete the San Diego fence and other barriers as authorized by Congress.

Historically, the construction of border fences usually results in strained diplomatic relations between the two nations and has environmental implications as well. In response to the passing of the Secure Fence Act of 2006, Mexican President Felipe Calderon compared the proposed US border fence to the Berlin Wall (Associated Press 2006). Many other nations including China, East Germany, Saudi Arabia, India, and Israel, have built border fences in response to illegal migration, counter-insurgencies, and for population containment. These and other border fencing projects have met with varying levels of success or failure but with added political ramifications. In the case of Saudi Arabia, the negative political repercussions resulted in the termination of the project (Feldner 2004). Border control has become "an optimal policy path because it offers a perceptually appealing political salve for an extraordinarily difficult set of problems that have no easy short-term solutions" (Andreas 2000, 147-148).

Primary Research Question

What is the terrorist deterrence or defeat effect of a fence on the US-Mexico border?

Secondary Research Questions

What type of terrorist would attempt a surreptitious crossing of the US land border?

What does a terrorist require to gain entrance into the US?

How could and how has a terrorist gained entrance into the US?

Why have terrorists historically not obtained entrance to the US via a surreptitious crossing of the US-Mexico border?

Why have terrorists crossed the US-Canada border instead of the US-Mexico border?

What would be the effects of increased regulation of immigration on illegal crossings?

Are current and planned specifications of the border fence necessary or sufficient to deter or defeat a terrorist attempting to cross illegally?

How has the fencing of portions of the US-Mexico border affected illegal immigration?

Significance

The securing of our nation's borders continues to be problematic in not only execution but in determining how to do it. The effect of a successful terrorist attack via a surreptitious border crossing could prove catastrophic. The construction of a border fence, its security, and maintenance require the allocation of many thousands of man hours and billions of dollars per year. With a continually prolonged period of stalled and limited funding of a mandated physical security barrier of the US-Mexico border, the Department of Defense (DOD) has had to pick up the tab in some of its security and construction. The DOD attempted to achieve this through the Corps of Engineers' and National Guard (NG) units' construction of border fencing, and by NG units providing administrative and observation security support. The tasking of these units to fill the gap is yet another requirement for DOD to fulfill in an environment of conflicting national needs and priorities. Many of the tasked units are already overburdened from deployments and preparation for deployments overseas or in response to natural disasters. The building of a border fence also creates political and cultural ramifications with divisions in the populace calling for the reinstatement of the original promise of security outlined in the Secure Fence Act of 2006 and Mexican national leaders comparing its construction to that of the Berlin Wall. Determining how or if a border fence should play a role in the security of our borders is essential to developing a focused and coordinated multinational and multi-agency mutually supportive border security plan.

Assumptions

A foreign terrorist is intelligent. Therefore, if attempting to conduct an attack on a target within the US that requires him or her to physically cross a US border, the terrorist will use the means to gain entrance that provides the greatest ease in movement and opportunity for success.

Limitations

The latest National Intelligence Estimate (NIE) stated that Al Qaeda poses the greatest terrorist threat to the US homeland. Although narco-terrorism has increased in frequency within Mexico and at border towns, criminally motivated terrorism will not be studied in relation to a US-Mexico border fence defeat or deterrence effect. In accordance with the NIE, the terrorist threat of this study will be limited to an Islamic fundamentalist terrorist organization or individual, such as Al Qaeda, an Al Qaeda trained terrorist, or a terrorist organization modeled after Al Qaeda.

CHAPTER 2

LITERATURE REVIEW

Introduction

In order to obtain a view of the entire body of the problem, the researcher must review a spectrum of related publications. In the case of the US-Mexico border fence, publications run the gamut, from emotionally laden opinion pieces, to politically inspired punditry and legislation, to "news worthy" headlines, to academic social analysis, and finally to sterile governmental reports. Emotions can run high, and these same emotions are often reflected in literature. The reaction among the general US populace to the construction of the US-Mexico border fence makes it a subject for both policy and politics, often with competing goals.

Just as one would conduct a dissection to understand the workings of the whole organism, the literature will be reviewed by categorizing it into different types to better understand the whole of the problem. The information reviewed will be discussed in five categories:

1. The Terrorist Threat

2. The Borders, Immigration, and Regional Terrorism

3. Border Security

4. US Legislation, Strategy, and Policy

5. Methodology

The Terrorist Threat

The National Intelligence Estimate (NIE), a Rand Corporation study, the Al Qaeda Manual, and a fictional novel are representative of the threat literature. The NIE, Rand Study, and novels are assessments of the capabilities, intents, and goals of terrorists while the Al Qaeda Manual is a method for operations.

NIEs are developed to provide policymakers with the most authoritative judgments on national security issues for the development of policies to protect US national security interests. These estimates are first developed by the relevant National Intelligence Officer and vetted by others in the intelligence community, with final approval provided by the National Intelligence Board. In July of 2007 the National Intelligence Board published the National Intelligence Estimate, The Terrorist Threat to the US Homeland. That estimate provided the US government's official judgment on the current terrorist threat to the US by stating that "Al Qaida is and will remain the most serious terrorist threat to the Homeland" (US National Intelligence Council 2007). The estimate additionally judged that Al Qaida will use its connections in Iraq to recruit more operatives, continue to attempt to attack targets to produce mass casualties, and continue to attempt to access weapons of mass destruction. In relation to the Western Hemisphere, the document stated that "the radical and violent segment of the West's Muslim population is expanding" (US National Intelligence Council 2007, The Terrorist Threat to the US Homeland).

Likewise a 2004 Rand Corporation terrorist assessment sponsored by the US Air Force listed Al Qaeda as the terrorist group with the greatest capability and hostility to carry out an attack against the US. In an assessment titled The Dynamic Terrorist Threat,

Rand intelligence analysts Kim Cragin and Sara A. Daly use the intuitive evaluation categories of motivation, benign to hostile, and capabilities, low to high, to rank twenty-two terrorist organizations as to their threat to the US. Additionally, the analysts use the Al Qaeda Manual to determine operational requirements for a terrorist (Cragin and Daly, 2004).

The Manchester (England) Metropolitan Police seized the Al Qaeda Manual during a search of an Al Qaeda member's home and subsequently used it as evidence during the trial of the Al Qaeda terrorist that bombed US Embassies in Africa. The document provides a "how to" manual for terrorists. The manual describes procedures for terrorists to follow for numerous tasks that the terrorist group would expect one of their operatives to be required to perform. Besides the usual rhetoric expected in an Islamic extremist journal, the manual provides instructions in eighteen lessons. The lessons include required characteristics for a cell member, how to gather information, and how to conduct actual attacks. In relation to the problem of this thesis, the manual discusses member qualifications, means to use forged documents, transportation, and establishing hiding places. Throughout the Al Qaeda training manual and specifically in reference to base locations, transportation, and general movement, it continually stresses the need to blend in with the environment and local populace (Al Qaeda Manual n.d., 1-180). A search for a complete publication of this manual was difficult as many of its postings were only excerpts. The US Department of Justice website posted a portion of the manual in 2005, but has since taken down the link. The posting is now maintained at the US Air Force Air University website, but it is missing lessons ten, and thirteen through seventeen. The posting is caveated with the statement that portions of the manual are missing to prevent the aiding or encouraging of future terrorists or acts of

terrorism. A complete copy of the manual was found at the Federation of American

Scientists website, however that copy was missing pages forty through seventy-nine. A

complete copy of the manual is maintained at the Smoking Gun website in html format.

Being a complete copy of the manual, The Smoking Gun's copy was used for this study.

The pages posted on that website were compared with those posted on two other websites

to verify accuracy, and no discrepancies were found between the pages posted on those

sites. However, it should be noted that pages sixty-eight to seventy-four, lesson ten,

could not be compared with the other postings for accuracy because those pages are only

available on The Smoking Gun's website.

   The fiction novel Pandora's Legion provides a possible scenario by which

terrorists traverse the US-Mexico border to gain entrance and conduct their attack within

the US. The plot entails the use of religious martyrs as human transports of a highly

communicable disease. The two martyrs fly to South America and then take a charter

flight to a Mexican safe house south of the US-Mexico border. They finally make their

way into the US via a drug smuggler who escorts them across the border (Coyle and

Tillman 2007). Although a work of fiction, past history has taught that fiction can

become non-fiction in reality. Many cite Tom Clancy's 1998 fictional work Executive

Orders as a prelude to the 9/11 terrorist attack in 2001.

The Borders, Immigration, and Regional Terrorism

   For the comparative analysis of Mexico and Canada, literature and online data

bases were used for a review of information relevant to terrorist operational requirements.

That review focused on the four subject categories of border characteristics, immigration demographics and law, and terrorism occurring within or originating from that country. The CIA World Factbook was accessed for general information on demographics, government composition, infrastructure and economy, and geographic boundaries, along with a brief description of transnational issues. The CIA World Factbook contains information on land border lengths with the US, Muslim populations, and transnational issues with the US (Mexico, Canada, CIA The World Factbook). Immigration policy of our border neighbors, Canada and Mexico, provide some insight into the potential support structure to persons attempting to enter the US via those two countries.

Because Mexican census data doesn't provide information on non-Christian religious traditions, further information on Muslim populations in Mexico was collected from two different studies and one article. An entry in the Jamestown Foundation's Terrorism Monitor estimates the number of Muslims in Mexico as two thousand. Of that number nearly all are Sunni and half of those can trace their ancestry to relatives that immigrated to Mexico at the end of the Ottoman Empire. It states that the recent scrutiny placed on this community because of suspicions that they may aid the infiltration of Islamic terrorists is misplaced and may divert attention away from areas of real threat (Zambellis 2006). Another study in the Institute for Islamic Study in the Modern World (ISIM) Review estimated the number of Muslims in Mexico at one thousand. The study further explores the movement of Islam in the country, where it is focused in the Chiapas region with the conversion of indigenous people. The study found that (Garvin 2005). Spiegel Online published an article on Islam in the Chiapas region. The article acknowledges that the Mexican government had sent secret service to the region under suspicion that the new Muslim converts among the indigenous people may be planning

13

subversive activity. However, it states that these Mayan Muslims have no interest in political extremism. The group had made an "ideological-religious alliance" with the Zapatistas in the Chiapas region, but that pact was primarily attributable to their more fundamental Islamic values that were contrary to the capitalist use of usury than any political motivation. The article further elaborates that the indigenous people of Mexico have provided the primary source for converts to non-Catholic religions, and consequently have received the persecution of the non-Catholics in Mexico (Glüsing 2005).

Dr. J. Michael Waller, a professor at The Institute of World Politics, has published two articles which provide insight on Mexico's immigration policy. The first focuses on how Mexico's constitution limits the rights of immigrants even after they have become naturalized citizens. Some of these limits are denial of property rights, ban from public political discourse, and expulsion from Mexico without reason or due process (Waller 2006, April). The second article focuses on Mexico's General Law on Population. Waller writes that this law allows for stiff fines and imprisonment as a felon for using false papers, attempting to re-enter Mexico after deportation, or failing to obey a deportation order (Waller 2006, May).

In April of 2007 the Council On Foreign Relations published a special report on illegal immigration from Mexico into the US. The report explores the issue of illegal immigration from an economic perspective to determine the driving factors and to evaluate US policy. Professor Hanson argues that illegal immigration provides more benefit to the economy than cost. Furthermore, Hanson predicts that unless a new worker program is implemented to provide the immigrant worker with a viable means to meet the

14

US economy's need for cheap labor, the Mexican worker will continue to cross illegally to provide that labor (Hanson 2007).

A review of literature on terrorism and violence in Mexico provides some understanding of counter-terrorism motivation of proponents of the US-Mexico border fence. In 2003 the Federal Research Division of the Library of Congress published a report on organized crime and terrorist activity in Mexico. The report discusses local insurgent and terrorist groups such as the Zapatistas and foreign terrorist organizations such as the FARC and ETA. However, the majority of the information in the report chronicles the activities of organized crime. The report found that much of the increased enforcement by the US government has brought about the dependence of organized crime on the use of tunnels and more sophisticated anti-detection methods. Additionally, US enforcement has increased dependence on human smugglers, making it second only to illicit drug trafficking in illegal profiting. The lack of information on local insurgent and local and foreign terrorist activity is due in large part to their lack of operations and increased enforcement against these groups by the Mexican government. Most local insurgent groups only number in the dozens and are mostly isolated to the southernmost Mexican states. While the report does cite statements by Mexican officials of Islamic extremist foreign terrorist organizations operating in the region, those statements were never substantiated or were denied by higher ranking officials of the Mexican government (Library of Congress 2003).

Two articles were found that substantiate the crackdown by the Mexican government against foreign terrorist organizations that had previously operated within Mexico. A 2008 Reuters article acknowledges Mexico's closure of a FARC supporters' office in the National Autonomous University of Mexico in 2002 (Lange 2008). The BBC reported that Mexican government had signed an extradition agreement with Spain in the mid-1990's, in effect agreeing to no longer treat ETA members as political refugees (BBC Online 2004).

A local borderland resident's view of Mexican narco-violence was obtained through the review of a detailed article posted on the Mexico Trucker Online blog site. The entry details which cartels are fighting for territory, the reasons behind their internal and external organizational conflict, and their fight against the government. That fight against the government, the blog author argues, has been brought about by the Mexican government's increased law enforcement efforts. However, without US cooperation to control demand, these efforts cannot rid Mexico of narco-trafficking. The blog author quotes the Director of the Texas Narcotics Officer Association as stating, "You have the president of Mexico [who] is doing something no other president has done before, that I can think of. He has basically declared war on the cartels." Additionally, the blog author writes that the Drug Enforcement Agency characterizes relations with Mexican authorities as at its best level ever (Mexican Trucker Online blog, entry posted June 2, 2008).

A series of articles by Reuters, the Associated Press, and the New York Times exemplify the increased violence by Mexican drug cartels. On September 15, 2008 a grenade was thrown into a crowd celebrating Mexican independence in the Mexican president's hometown of Morelia, killing eight people (Garcia 2008). Traci Carl's article quotes the US ambassador as stating that the drug cartels in Mexico had crossed a line from endangering bystanders to intentionally targeting civilians (Carl 2008). In response to the government's accusations against them, some of the drug cartels went as far as to conduct their own information campaign through text messages to reporters and by hanging banners around Morelia (Lacey 2008). Although denied by the suspected drug cartel, suspects involved with the cartel have been captured and have confessed their involvement (Rodriguez 2008). Mexican prosecutors stated that the three suspects were members of the Zetas, a group of hit men, that work for the Gulf cartel (Wilkinson 2008).

The review of literature to gather information on Canada's analysis consisted of sources similar to those used for the analysis of Mexico. In order to obtain comparable information, additional Canadian Muslim demographic data beyond the scope of the CIA World Factbook was obtained through the Canadian Census website. Unlike the Mexican census data, the Canadian census contains data on Muslim population numbers. The website also provides links to additional studies conducted using census data. Specifically, data was obtained that showed numbers of Muslims by province, which included in some cases the increase in that province's Muslim population over the past ten years, and their predominant location of residency within that province. Data from this study of 2001 census data showed that major Muslim populations were only found in five provinces. Each of these provinces saw large increases in Muslim populations over the past ten years, four out of those five saw their Muslim population double. All of these populations of Muslims were predominantly concentrated in major cities, and sixty-one percent of the total Muslim population of Canada resides in Toronto (Provincial and Territorial Highlights, Religions in Canada, Census of Canada 2001). Canada's immigration policy is primarily governed by two acts, the Immigration Act of 1976 and the Immigration and Refugee Act of 2002. The 1976 Act removed the requirements of applicants to be of European origin. The 2002 Act enhanced the points system for entry to facilitate the entry of "skilled" workers. Information on these and other pieces of Canadian Immigration Law and policy were obtained through a website ran by Canadiana.org. This website provides a chronology of immigration law and policy in Canada, along with links to scanned copies of the legislative documents (Specific Events & Topics, Immigration Acts 1866-2001, Canada in the Making).

The Council On Foreign Relations published an article analyzing Canadian immigration policy in 2006. The author cites the 2006 UN Report on International Migration and Development's ranking of Canada as seventh among the top twenty-eight countries that host seventy-five percent of all international immigrants. This fact has much to do with Canada's liberal policy on immigration. The article states that the Canadian Immigration and Refugee Protection Act, 2001, provided new restrictions on appealing claims for asylum and empowered authorities to deport individuals based upon suspicion of a security threat. However, any immigrant may still apply for asylum and travel around the country while awaiting their determination. Additionally, Canada has historically granted fifty percent of its applicants refugee status whereas the US has comparatively granted thirty-five percent. As a result of this liberal immigration policy, Canada's Muslim population had increased to 750,000 from 580,000 in 2001, ninety percent of those migrating from South Asian and Arab countries (Smick 2006).

Information on terrorism in or originating from Canada was obtained through several news articles and a US Department of Justice, Office of the Inspector General Report. Abu Mezer is the first terrorist known to have entered the US from Canada. The New York Times published an article in 1997 recounting his infiltration of the US and final apprehension. Upon entry into Canada and application for political asylum he traveled to Toronto, Ontario. Abu Mezer twice hiked across the border from Canada via the Cascade Mountains in Northwest Washington, and crossed a third time using a bus. He was apprehended each time and on the third attempt was turned down for political asylum by Canada. He was granted stay in the US once he dropped his appeal during his hearing and agreed to voluntarily leave the country by August 23, 1997. During each attempt he was apprehended but allowed to stay in the US upon appealing for political asylum. Authorities from both sides of the border were surprised that he was apprehended at all during his crossings due to the huge expanse of the area and sparsely monitored region. He was later wounded with his accomplice in a New York Police raid of his apartment where items for pipe bombs designed to target New York subways were found, three weeks prior to his agreed upon date of departure from the US (Egan 1997).

The Office of the Inspector General under the US Department of Justice published a detailed report on how two illegal immigrants, Gazi Ibrahim Abu Mezer and Lafi Khalil, entered and remained in the US prior to their arrest in New York for the New York subway bombing plot. Khalil was eventually acquitted of all charges and was subsequently deported. The report details the three apprehensions and processing of Abu Mezer, along with the actions of various government agencies involved (US Department of Justice 1998).

Abu Mezer entered Canada on September 14, 1993 under a student visa from Israel. Less than two weeks later Mezer applied for a non-immigrant visa to the US and was denied. In November of 1993 Mezer then applied for refugee status in Canada and a hearing in 1994 found sufficient cause for his formal application. His status as a refugee was still pending at the time of the investigation regardless of his two criminal arrests in Canada and his arrest in the US. According a Canadian immigration official, "a serious criminal offense in Canada would not affect Mezer's ability to receive CR [refugee] status" (US Department of Justice 1998, sec. II A-C).

Mezer was first apprehended on June 23, 1996 by a park ranger in a remote wilderness area in North Cascades National Park after Mezer had signaled some tourists for assistance. Mezer and his accomplice had hiked through the park from the Canadian side and were exhibiting signs of hypothermia. The two were transferred to USBP custody and the official arrest report commented that Mezer was under suspicion of alien smuggling. This comment was based upon Canadian immigration information stating that Mezer had previously been connected with smuggling in Manitoba, Canada. A criminal history check on the two revealed no criminal history, and as was customary policy the two were voluntarily returned to Canada (US Department of Justice 1998, sec. II D 2.b.)

Mezer's second apprehension occurred on June 29, 1996 approximately sixty-five miles west of his previous apprehension when he jogged into the US near the Blaine sector POE from an adjoining large open park. The apprehending USBP agent returned Mezer to Canada after Canadian authorities confirmed his refugee status and agreed to accept him. After returning Mezer to Canadian authorities the apprehending USBP agent learned of Mezer's previous history of "alien smuggling" and revised his report. This report led the intelligence section of the border sector to distribute a report to the INS and FBI, stating that the event could be the first instance of middle-eastern alien smuggling in the Blaine sector (US Department of Justice 1998, sec. II D 2.c.).

A USBP agent apprehended Mezer during his third attempt on January 14, 1997 twenty-five miles south of the US-Canada border at a bus station in Bellingham, Washington. Mezer was arrested with two other middle-eastern males. The agent entered Mezer into deportation proceedings after learning that Canadian officials would probably not accept him back based upon his past history. After several hearings Mezer's bond was reduced from $15,000 to $5,000, which he posted after completing his request for asylum in the US. The individual posting the bond was actually an illegal immigrant who had overstayed his visa, but INS policy did not require a background check on individuals posting bond at that time. The judge also submitted Mezer's application to the US State Department for review of the claim since Mezer did admit that he had been associated with Hamas by Israeli authorities. The US State Department could not confirm that they had done the review and further stated that it wasn't their responsibility to ensure the validity of the claim (US Department of Justice 1998, sec. II E 1-7.).

Mezer did show up for his April 7th hearing in Seattle, but because of the length required for the hearing it was rescheduled for January 20, 1998. After a review of the new procedures mandated by the Executive Office of Immigration Review prior to the April 7th hearing, a new hearing was rescheduled again for June 23, 1997. On June 1, 1997 Mezer informed his attorney that he had moved to New York and wanted his case transferred to that jurisdiction, but subsequently decided to withdraw his application on June 11, 1997 after further legal advice. On June 14 Mezer falsely informed his attorney that he was in Canada. At the June 23rd hearing the judge eventually ordered a sixty day period for voluntary departure with mandatory deportation after that period since they could not validate Mezer's claim for leaving the US. Mezer was shot in a police raid of his apartment on July 31, 1997 (US Department of Justice 1998, sec. II E 6-12).

The report also investigated the conditions and procedures conducted in the Blaine sector. It noted at that time that more aliens are apprehended in that sector than any other sector along the US-Canada border. Additionally of note, the Chief Border Patrol Agent of the Blaine sector stated that decreases in apprehensions in his sector were due to the detailing of manpower out of his sector to the southern border (US Department of Justice 1998, sec. II D 2a).

The Seattle Times published a series of seventeen articles detailing Ahmed Ressam's story, from his childhood and motivation to leave his homeland in Algeria to his illegal immigration through several countries and subsequent apprehension in the US. Ahmed Ressam, one of the Millennium Bombing terrorists, attempted to smuggle bomb making materials in his vehicle through the US POE at Port Angeles, Washington. Ressam had traveled to Montreal in 1994 using a falsified passport. Although he admitted that the passport was fraudulent during questioning, he was allowed to stay in Canada under his own recognizance after claiming political asylum. Ressam spent the next two years collecting welfare and stealing in Montreal, selling stolen IDs to a documents procurer for Islamic terrorists. During that time he was arrested twice for stealing. The first time he was ordered to leave the country, but Ressam never showed up for his deportation. When arrested for the second time, three months after his deportation date, he was fined and put on probation for two years. By 1998 Ressam had been influenced enough by his Islamic associates to obtain another fraudulent identity and Canadian passport to travel to Afghanistan to train with Al Qaeda. After his training and receiving finance for his plot, Ressam returned to Vancouver, Canada via Seoul, Korea and Los Angeles. It was during this transit of the Los Angeles airport that Ressam chose that airport as his target. For the next ten months Ressam traveled in Canada under his new identity and prepared to carry out his plot to blow up the Los Angeles airport. The plot ended with his apprehension on December 14, 1999 by US Customs Officers (Bernton, Carter, Heath, and Neff 2002, Chapters 1-17).

The articles further recount the efforts of investigators for the US, Canada, and France, and their successes and failures in cooperative counter-terrorism operations. Although French law enforcement had made several different requests to investigate or apprehend members of a suspected Islamic terrorist cell in Montreal, Canadian officials continually delayed any action by their investigators. Delayed Canadian intelligence surveillance of Ressam and other individuals participating in the Montreal group for over two years never lead to apprehensions or transfer of that information to the US or France. However, the apprehension of Ressam brought about new cooperation between the US and European counter-terrorism organizations. Unfortunately, internal problems within the FBI prevented the use of French intelligence in the apprehension of a French national Zacarias Moussaoui prior to September 11, 2001 (Bernton, Carter, Heath, and Neff 2002, Chapters 1-17).

The most recent incident of Islamic terrorism in Canada occurred in 2006. An Associated Press article published in USA Today recounts the apprehension of seventeen Al Qaeda inspired terror suspects in Toronto, Canada. The group had obtained three tons of ammonium nitrate and related bomb making materials, and was charged with numerous terrorism charges. The assistant Royal Canadian Mounted Police commissioner stated that the "group posed a real and serious threat," and "had the capacity and intent to carry out these attacks". Additionally, according to the assistant director of operations for the Canadian Security Intelligence Service, the group "appeared to have become adherents of a violent ideology inspired by Al Qaeda" (Associated Press, 2006)

In 2004 the Anti-Defamation League published an article that reported on the current and past terrorist and terrorist related activities in Canada. The article states that terrorists have been using Canada as a support base to facilitate travel into other countries, recruit new agents in the immigrant communities, raise capital through front organizations, and procure weapons. The Canadian Security Intelligence Service (CSIS) is quoted as stating "terrorists have moved 'from significant support roles, such as fundraising and procurement, to actually planning and preparing terrorist acts from Canadian territory'". Additionally the CSIS is quoted, "they [terrorist] abuse Canada's immigration, pass-port, welfare, and charity regulations". The article also acknowledges security agreements between the US and Canada and the development of additional Integrated Border Enforcement Teams. Canada has also designated thirty-four terrorist organizations, frozen their assets, and outlawed the membership or fundraising for any of these groups. The article also notes that Canada and the US share the longest international border in the world. The known activities of Al Qaeda, Hezbollah, Hamas, Sikh extremism, and Tamil extremism are detailed in this article as well (Anti-Defamation League 2004).

<u>Border Security</u>

Although numerous studies on border security have been conducted, the review of that literature focused on those specifically related to the US-Canada and US-Mexico borders. This literature review included official government agency reports, academic works, news articles, a television documentary, and even opinion pieces or punditry. Finally, this author includes the information obtained during his attendance of the 2008 Border Security Conference at the University of Texas at El Paso.

The Government Accountability Office (GAO) and Congressional Research Service (CRS) have published the preponderance of official reports on border security. These reports, usually initiated by a request from Congress, are generally unbiased in their reporting and provide statuses on areas of interests with issues for consideration by Congress. While conclusions are generally left to the reader, findings are provided in these reports.

In January of 2007 the GAO published a report detailing the status of progress in addressing the security vulnerabilities exposed by the 9/11 attacks. The GAO found that much progress had been made in improving screening procedures of airline passengers and in using the visa process as a tool to combat terrorism. While the majority of the report focused on commercial aviation security and visa related policies, the report did review management and organizational efforts by DHS. In regards to management of the department, the GAO found that "developing and implementing a risk-based framework to balance trade-offs between security and other priorities remains a critical strategic federal challenge". This finding referred to statements not only reflected in the 2002 National Strategy for Homeland Security, but also to presidential directives and statements made by the Secretary of DHS. According to the GAO, the development and implementation of a "risk-based framework" by DHS is critical to ensure the threat focused investment of limited national resources to strengthen security (US Government Accountability Office 2007).

The type of terrorist threat that could come from Canada was tested in a GAO investigation in 2007. The investigators found that "a determined cross-border violator would likely be able to bring radioactive materials or other contraband undetected in the United States by crossing the US-Canada border at any of the locations we investigated" (US Government Accountability Office, Kutz 2007, 12). For the US-Canada border portion of the investigation, the investigators identified four locations using publically available information. All crossing sites were readily accessible from a state road and appeared unmonitored.

At three of the four locations, an investigator simulated the carrying of radioactive materials by using a duffle bag and mock radioactive materials inside the bag. The investigator generally remained in the area where he had crossed for at least fifteen minutes. Only one of the simulated crossings brought about a response from the USBP after they had received a call from a concerned citizen, but the agent never found the investigators even though they had parked nearby to observe traffic at the POE. At one of the three sites the investigator conducted the simulated crossing at four different locations in that area. At the one site where a simulated crossing was not conducted investigators found six locations where a state road ended at the border and photographed the area, again with no response from USBP (US Government Accountability Office, Kutz 2007, 3-6).

The investigators also identified several POEs with posted daytime hours and photographed the POE after the posted hours to determine if there would be a response from the USBP. The investigators determined during their surveillance that although the road for the POE was gated that they could have easily driven around it. When no response had occurred after twelve minutes, the investigators drove South three miles and were finally pulled over by USBP. The investigators indicated to the agent that they were federal investigators testing border security and the agent let them go without asking for identification, although one of the investigators briefly flashed a badge (US Government Accountability Office, Kutz 2007, 7).

The same GAO investigation also tested border security on the US-Mexico border. As stated previously in the Canadian portion of this investigation, most of the investigation focused on crossing at locations that appeared not to be monitored and or physically more favorable to crossing by foot with quick access from a road. Consequently, the agents did not attempt to cross at a location where pedestrian type of fencing had been constructed. As was the case with their US-Canada border crossing attempts, the GAO used publicly available information and limited surveillance to determine locations to conduct the simulated crossings. The GAO noticed that there wasn't a large presence of National Guard and USBP in federally managed areas adjacent to the US-Mexico border and identified two locations between two different states to conduct their investigation. A preliminary site was additionally identified to test border security reaction to the investigator's actions (US Government Accountability Office, Kutz 2007, 7-8).

The preliminary site identified was a quarter of a mile from a US-Mexico POE along a dirt road that paralleled the border. While traveling to the site the investigators passed USBP agents and National Guard units and observed UAVs and helicopters. The investigators stopped their vehicle approximately three quarters of a mile from the last observed USBP vehicles and walked to the US-Mexico border (see figure below). After fifteen minutes the investigator returned to the vehicle and drove back to the main road. During the hour that the investigators were in the area they had not observed any public traffic on that road and were not questioned by law enforcement personnel. When US Customs and Border Protection (CBP) was questioned about the event, investigators were informed that there was no expectation that their actions would be questioned since they'd approached the border from the US side (US Government Accountability Office, Kutz 2007, 8-9).

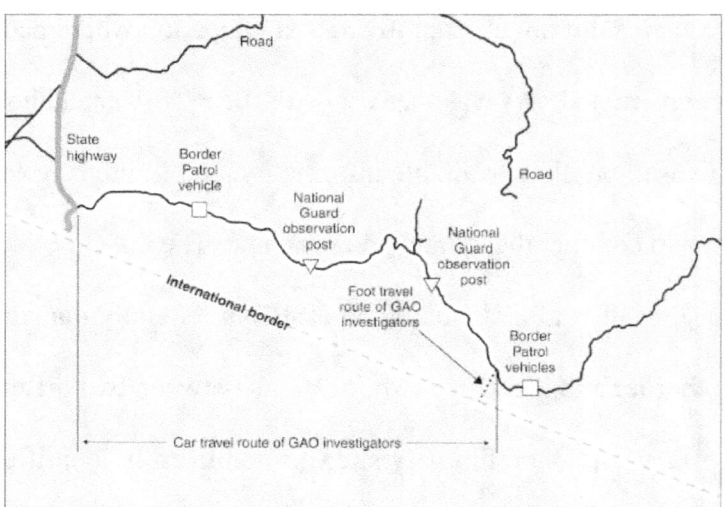

Figure 3.   Route of GAO Investigators at U.S.-Mexico Border Location
Source: GAO, *BORDER SECURITY, Security Vulnerabilities at Unmanned and Unmonitored U.S. Border Locations* (Location: GAO, September 27, 2007), 9

The first location investigated on federal land was located parallel to a road that a visitor center employee had stated was closed due to fence construction. The investigators proceeded down this road and pulled off to the side close to a border vehicle barrier. One of the investigators exited the vehicle and crossed over the vehicle barrier into Mexico, and subsequently returned to determine if their actions would be detected. Although the investigators remained at the location for fifteen minutes, they observed no response by law enforcement personnel (US Government Accountability Office, Kutz 2007, 9-10). As a vehicle border barrier is designed to require the illegal immigrant to cross on foot and remain on foot for a period of time sufficient to allow law enforcement personnel to interdict, fifteen minutes may have been outside of their response parameters. However, the GAO investigators could not obtain any evidence that their actions had been detected. The CBP response to their investigation was that jurisdictional issues as well as resource restrictions prevented their response to all instances of suspicious activity on federal lands (US Government Accountability Office, Kutz 2007, 11).

The second location, also on federal lands, involved two areas where previous border crossing activity had been identified. Investigators located foot paths and matching boat ramps on both sides of the river and remained at the location for over ninety minutes. The investigators also observed no monitoring or response by law enforcement personnel at the location as was the case at the previous location (US Government Accountability Office, Kutz 2007, 10-11).

In 2007 the GAO published a report on the implementation of the Secure Border Initiative Program. The GAO found that the USBP had met its goal of seventy miles of border fencing with an average cost of $2.9 million per mile, but the current plan to use contractors to finish the remaining portions of the fence could increase the estimated cost. Additionally, the USBP's ability to determine resources required in each border sector were hindered because SBInet, the Boeing developed advanced surveillance system, had not become operational (US Government Accountability Office, Stana 2007).

Many of the same findings in were presented in the GAO's 2008 report on border security programs and operations. However, this report focused more on operations at POEs. The GAO found that a lack of infrastructure and numbers of officers has hindered CBP's ability to thoroughly inspect travelers and detect fraudulent documents. Several instances of officers failing to carry out inspections in accordance with CBP policy were video-taped even after CBP had taken directed management to correct similar past failures (US Government Accountability Office, Stana 2008, 5). Additionally, shortages of inspection staff prevented the operation of radiation monitors and other inspection technology, and prevented the training of staff on the operation of new equipment (US Government Accountability Office, Stana 2008, 6-7). Identification of fraudulent documents was lacking at primary inspection stations at POEs because the technology required to verify electronic passports and fingerprint data on border crossing cards were located at secondary inspection stations. Additionally, officers at primary inspection did not routinely send individuals with border crossing cards to secondary inspection to verify their fingerprint data (US Government Accountability Office, Stana 2008, 7). The program designed to track the entrance and exit of foreign national visitors to the US, the U.S. Visitor and Immigrant Status Indicator Technology (US-VISIT), still does not have the operational capability to track the exit of these visitors (US Government

Accountability Office, Stana 2008, 11). The GAO also reported that the training of the planned increase of 6,000 additional USBP agents could prove problematic as experienced agents were planned for transfer to the Canadian border (US Government Accountability Office, Stana 2008, 16).

The majority of information on border security of the US-Mexico border and specifically on the border fence issue has been produced by the Congressional Research Service (CRS) in three reports. These reports provide data on trends of numbers of apprehensions of illegal immigrants attempting to cross the US-Mexico border, status of border barriers, and analysis of the effects of border barriers on illegal immigration. The first report provides much of the data that was used in the other two for further analysis.

The 2005 CRS report on the role of the USBP provides an overview of the history and development of the agency. The report states that the USBP transitioned to a focused strategy on counter-terrorism after 9/11 while still maintaining its mission to prevent illegal immigration (Library of Congress 2005, 4-5). By July of 2004, the USBP had tripled the number of agents on the Canadian border to 983 agents. This still only equates to less than ten percent of the USBP agent manpower, and reflects its emphasis on cooperation with Canadian authorities and dependence upon surveillance equipment to secure that border. Apprehension data for the US-Canada and US-Mexico border are both analyzed, however the report warns against using that data to determine correlations in migration patterns or enforcement. This is due to the fact that apprehensions are numbers of apprehension events instead of numbers of individuals, the data does not account for individuals that cross multiple times, and estimates of illegal immigrants in the US do not take into account how they arrived (Library of Congress 2005, 8-9).

Apprehension data for the northern border shows a relatively stable number apprehension from 2002 to 2004, while enforcement hours more than doubled over the same period. The report suggests that this may be reflective of the USBP's focus on terrorist infiltration along that border instead of illegal immigration (Library of Congress 2005, 19-20). The 9/11 Commission report is also cited in the report and its criticisms of USBP policy in securing the Canadian border. The report poses the question to Congress of whether or not the USBP's increase in manpower on the northern border adequately addresses the commission's criticisms (Library of Congress 2005, 22).

Apprehension data for the US-Mexico border shows an increase in apprehensions in more remote sectors of the border over time. This increase in apprehensions in sectors with fewer assigned agents and border barriers suggests a migration of illegal immigrants away from more heavily enforced sectors (Library of Congress 2005, 11-12). However, the report also discusses the tripling of USBP agents deployed to the Tucson sector from 1994 to 1999 where apprehensions also significantly increased during that period (Library of Congress 2005, 14).

The 2007 CRS report on the San Diego Fence explores the issues of the first congressionally authorized fence on the US-Mexico border. This report also analyzes apprehension data, but focuses that analysis on the San Diego sector. Numbers of apprehensions in the San Diego sector steadily declined. This decline coincided with the combination of the increase in fencing, numbers of agents, more advanced equipment, and the passage of the Immigration Reform and Immigrant Responsibility Act of 1996 (IIRIRA) (Library of Congress 2007, 4). The report also notes the coinciding increases in apprehensions in the Tucson sector at that time, and USBP's stance that the reductions in apprehensions in the San Diego sector demonstrate the effectiveness of their deterrent strategy.

The 2008 CRS report on barriers along the US international border has been updated as required from its initial publication in 2006. As the San Diego Fence is the longest standing border barrier, it is the focus of the portion of the study dedicated to determining effectiveness of border fencing. Another USBP sector along the US-Mexico border is the Tucson Sector. The Tucson sector at the time of the study was not fenced, and consequently was included in the study to compare it to the San Diego Sector. While there are other non-fenced sectors that could have been chosen for comparison, it appears that the Tucson Sector was chosen because it provided a more notable change in numbers of apprehensions in comparison to the decreases in the San Diego Sector.

Although recently updated, the portion of the study analyzing apprehensions in the San Diego Sector only covers the period of 1992 to 2004. CRS obtained and analyzed CBP records of numbers of apprehensions during this period and compared these apprehension between areas in the San Diego Sector and the Tucson Sector as a whole (Library of Congress 2008, 16). During this period not only was the San Diego Fence primary fence completed and its secondary fencing initiated, but enforcement was also increased. Operation Gatekeeper was initiated in October of 1994 when the USBP determined that the primary fence was having little effect on curbing immigration. The operation entailed a three-tiered positioning of USBP agents and an increase of at least 150% in man-power, electronic sensors, vehicles, and night-vision goggles (Library of Congress 2008, 3).

The possible political ramifications resulting from the construction of a border

fence are exemplified by Saudi Arabia's dismantling of its border fence with Yemen

(Feldner 2004), and by Mexican President Calderon's comparison of the US-Mexico

border fence to the Berlin Wall (Associated Press 2006). Fox News reported on a

smuggling route on the Arizona border gaining the local name of the "Arab Road" and

related it to Congressman Tancredo's statement that USBP apprehension records show

the apprehension of 132 nationals from countries considered a security threat (Fox News

2005). A Yuma Sun article demonstrated the adaptation of smugglers to increased

enforcement by reporting on the arrest of an individual for digging a cross border tunnel

in 2008 (Gilbert 2008). The use of tunnels to subvert increased law enforcement was also

demonstrated by the discovery of a tunnel in Calexico, California. That tunnel was one

of seven found in the Calexico area in the past few years (Marosi 2008). Finally, two San

Francisco Chronicle articles, one in 2006 and another in 2007, provided an alternate cost

analysis by exploring the cost of constructing a border fence as written in the House

version of the Secure Fence Act of 2006 (Hendricks 2006), and after signing of the bill

into law (Hendricks 2007).

Peter Andreas, Assistant Professor of Political Science at Reed College, wrote

War Games: Policing the U.S.-Mexico Divide, prior to 9/11 that still provides valid

insight into why the US polices the border the way in which it does. Andreas argues that

the law enforcement conducted along the border is more of a high profile display of force

for political reasons instead of a really effective means of dealing with the complex

problems on the border. He also states that the focus of US efforts should be on decreasing the demand for illegal labor and drugs in order to obtain control of the border (Andreas 2000).

Tony Payan, Assistant Professor of International Relations and Foreign Policy at the University of Texas at El Paso, wrote *The Three U.S.-Mexico Border Wars* post 9/11. In that book Payan examines the history of the U.S.-Mexico border and the three wars he argues govern the border today, and how the residents of the borderland deal with the increasingly restrictive environment in response to these wars. Payan provides many anecdotal examples of the effects of border security on the people of the "borderland" through personal observation and interviews. He investigates the human smuggling of illegal immigrants by posing as a buyer, and interviews a former drug smuggler. Payan details in his book his approach of a coyote who quoted him prices to smuggle people of different ethnic backgrounds across the border. Interestingly it would cost more to smuggle a Cuban than a Middle Easterner, $6,000 to $1,000 comparatively (Payan 2006, 69). The interviewed drug smuggler informs him that a drug smuggler would not smuggle a terrorist into the US because it doesn't make good business sense.

Payan argues that the economic state of Mexico has provided the motivation for illegal immigration. This depressed economic state along with the increased enforcement against drug trafficking in the Caribbean and an ineffective effort to decrease demand, facilitated the movement of drug trafficking into Mexico. The ungoverned US-Mexico border and Mexico's large pool of unemployed citizens provided a prime opportunity for re-establishing their illegal trade (Payan 2006, 25-28). Increased law enforcement along the border to stop illegal immigration has had a similar effect as that of law enforcement to stop drug smuggling. Law enforcement has increased the dependence of the illegal

35

immigrant on human smugglers to cross the border and has pushed that immigration to less enforced areas (Payan 2006, 59, 69-70). Payan also states that the same increased law enforcement has required illegal immigrants to become more dependent on the coyote in order to cross the US-Mexico border. Consequently, that dependence has provided the coyote with the funds to increase his capabilities (Payan 2006, 69-71)

In summation of his analysis, Payan believes that the only solution to the border security problem is a bi-national strategy with Mexico along with its economic and political reform on par with Canada. To accomplish this Payan proposes the establishment of a bi-lateral or tri-lateral institutional mechanism like the European Commission to identify common North American problems and further cooperation on economic, social, diplomatic, and law enforcement efforts (Payan 2006).

A "National Geographic Explorer" broadcast titled *Border Wars* documented illegal immigration along the US-Mexico border. The program explored the support infrastructure for illegal immigrants, USBP law enforcement efforts, and humanitarian aid provided for illegal immigrants crossing in remote areas. USBP's heightened enforcement was accredited with the movement of illegal immigrants to more remote areas. The program stated that in the summer it takes an average male fifty gallons of water to make the three day trip from the crossing site to Tucson on foot. Consequently, the mortality rate for illegal immigrants has increased and Tucson has had to build a new facility to store remains and hire a full time forensic scientist. Additionally, the efforts of smugglers to negate increased enforcement in the San Diego sector were demonstrated by a USBP agent's telling of the discovery of several tunnels, one which was dug eight-five feet below the surface to avoid ground surveillance radar (National Geographic Explorer, originally aired on the National Geographic Channel, November 12, 2008).

Unfortunately, much of the non-government produced literature dedicated to the study of US border security, and especially US-Mexico border security, is politically motivated. Although the literature has a biased approach, most of the stated opinions are backed by citations which can provide the unbiased researcher with valuable data for further analysis. Three of these types of books were reviewed as a part of this thesis.

Michelle Malkin, a syndicated columnist and political pundit for the conservative right, wrote *Invasion* in 2002 to bring to light the vulnerabilities of the US Immigration system to terrorist manipulation to gain entrance into the US. Her book provides information on how terrorists gain entrance into the US and suggestions on what should be done to eliminate these vulnerabilities. She argues that the movement against immigration reform legislation was formed by ethnically self-identified activists backed by profit motivated lawyers to prevent what they perceive as racist legislation. She advocates abolishing the immigration court system, converting closed military bases into detention facilities for awaiting deportees, and posting armed NG units on the border until 100,000 new USBP and INS agents can be deployed (Malkin 2002).

Tom Tancredo, US Congressman from Colorado, has written a book which warns of the impending terrorist threat if our borders are not soon closed and secured. This book, In Mortal Danger, focuses on Congressman Tancredo's perceived threat to American culture by increasing numbers of illegal immigrants from Mexico. Congressman Tancredo states that terrorists are readily infiltrating in the US through the US-Mexico border based upon apprehension statistics showing increases in OTMs (Other

Than Mexican) apprehended since 9/11. He argues that the immigration enforcement system has consistently shown that it is incapable of managing legal immigration which demonstrates that it would not be capable of managing a guest worker program. He advocates making English the official language, ending the current guest worker program, ending birth right citizenship for illegal aliens, and posting military troops on the border (Tancredo 2006).

Patrick Buchanan, former presidential candidate and Republican pundit, has been a long time advocate of building a barrier between the US and Mexico even before the 9/11 attack. In his book *State of Emergency*, Buchanan argues that the American Southwest is being conquered by Mexico via an invasion of illegal Mexican immigrants. Although politically motivated and focused on the issue of illegal immigration it provides interesting insight into the way many opponents of immigration tie into their argument the need for national security from a terrorist threat. Often these opponents equate illegal immigration to vulnerability in homeland defense (Buchanan 2006).

The author attended the 2008 Border Security Conference and collected two days of audio tape of prepared speeches by guest speakers and their responses to questions from the audience. The conference was held as a public forum at the University of Texas at El Paso and sponsored by several commercial industries specializing in surveillance, information analysis, and data processing technologies. The agenda of the conference was structured with opening remarks for each day, five key speakers, and four panels of speakers, each panel covering a subject area.

The first day covered the subjects of integrating technology and border contraband. Key addresses were provided by Michael J. Sullivan, Acting Director of

Alcohol, Tobacco, Firearms and Explosives, Robert S. Mueller, Director of Federal Bureau of Investigation (FBI), and Mexican Consul General in El Paso, Ambassador Roberto Rodriguez Hernandez. The first panel of speakers predominantly comprised of business executives from the different sponsors. They discussed what products they provide and how they integrate support security operations. Besides the speakers from the sponsor businesses, the predominant theme of discussion revolved around dealing with organized crime in Mexico and facilitating the movement of trade while preventing the smuggling of illicit items through Ports of Entry (POEs). Mueller stated that the three main areas of concern on the border were drugs, human smuggling, and gang activity. Sullivan discussed the issue of preventing the smuggling of weapons from the US to Mexico, citing that ninety to ninety-five percent of the weapons confiscated are from the US, two-thirds of which originated in Texas. Ambassador Rodriguez also recognized the rising violence in Mexico and past problems with corruption. He commented on how many of his associates in Ciudad Juárez were adverse to meeting him for dinner on that side of the border, they no longer left their residences after dark because of the violence. He further re-emphasized the points made by acting Director Sullivan in regard to US weapon involvement in narco-violence, and President Calderon's commitment to fight the drug cartels. Additionally, he emphasized the importance of the Merida Initiative as not only a symbol of security cooperation between Mexico and the US, but also a necessary partnership to effectively deal with organized crime in the region.

The second day covered the subjects of educating national security professionals, first panel, and effective trade and commerce, second panel. Key addresses were provided by LTG William Webster, NORTHCOM Deputy Commanding Officer, and W.

Ralph Basham, Commissioner of Customs and Border Protection. LTG Webster commented that NORTHCOM daily responds to upwards of forty incidents. He stated that some of those incidents could be homeland security issues, but did not provide further insight with examples or how many of these incidents were related to homeland security. The first panel discussed the formation of the National Center for Border Security and Immigration. This center combines the efforts of several universities and agencies for the research dedicated to border security and the education of college students preparing for careers in homeland security. The second panel focused on the competing issues of border security and efficient flow of goods through POEs. The inadequacy and aging infrastructure at POEs was the main issue identified during the discussion. Maria Luisa O'Connell, President of the Border Trade Alliance, mentioned the importance of the Merida Initiative in improving the speed of goods across the border. Specifically, she emphasized the importance of US support to providing inspection equipment and training to Mexican security officials to allow for the increased clearance of goods prior to reaching the border.

The author did pose questions to the panel covering border contraband, the panel most related to the issues of a terrorist threat and the security of the US-Mexico border. Specifically, the questions of how the increase in apprehensions of OTMs influences the current terrorist threat assessment, and how the use of a border fence facilitated border security against a terrorist threat were posed. The response by that panel was that they wanted to remain on topic, and that the question didn't apply to the issues they were covering.

US Legislation, Strategy, and Policy

Legislation and policy provide the framework upon which the current construction and operation of the US-Mexico border fence has taken shape. Legislation provides a base from which one can attempt to obtain a stated purpose for the building of the border fence along with guidelines contracted into law by which the responsible parties must operate. The two main legislative acts that govern the construct of the US-Mexico border fence are the 2006 Secure Fence Act and the 2007 Omnibus Appropriations Bill. The 2006 Secure Fence Act provides the purpose for the US-Mexico border fence by defining operational control.

In this section, the term 'operational control' means the prevention of all unlawful entries into the United States, including entries by terrorists, other unlawful aliens, instruments of terrorism, narcotics, and other contraband.(Secure Fence Act 2006, 1)

The wording of the Act also demonstrates the emphasis on combating terrorism, thus providing validity to the analysis of the US-Mexico border fence as an effective mechanism for the prevention of terrorist entrance into the US. Additionally, the Secure Fence Act mandated the type, length, and location of the border fence (Secure Fence Act 2006, 2). The Consolidated Appropriations Act of 2008, also known as the 2007 Omnibus Bill, finally provided the initial funding for the border fence while revising the requirements on its type, length, and location. By providing the purpose and guidelines for the border fence construction, a model of the proposed border fence can be developed for the assessment of its efficacy in preventing the entrance of a terrorist into the US.

Although the proposed immigration reform acts from 2005 to 2007 never passed into law, they provide some insight into the differing viewpoints on strategy to secure the

41

US-Mexico border. In 2005 and 2006 both houses of congress drafted bills for immigration reform that only passed in their originating house. H.R. 4437, *Border Protection, Anti-terrorism, and Illegal Immigration Control Act of 2005*, focused on additional border enforcement while criminalizing illegal immigrants and those that aid them (US House 2005, H 4437). S.2611, *Comprehensive Immigration Reform Act of 2006*, focused on establishing a means to obtain citizenship for illegal immigrants already within the US, and a security enhanced guest worker program with a mandate of half the border fence length proposed in H.R. 4437 (US Senate 2006, S 2611).

US strategy and policy to defeat and deter terrorism are laid out in two main documents. The first is the 2007 *National Strategy for Homeland Security* (NSHS), and the second is the 2005 *National Strategy for Combating Terrorism*. Neither document specifically mentions the use of border barriers or the construction of a border fence. In applicability to border security, the 2005 *National Strategy for Combating Terrorism* only briefly mentions inhibiting terrorists from crossing US borders and improving border security. This task is categorized under the short term priority of action of "Prevent attacks by terrorist networks" (US National Security Council 2005, 11-13). The 2007 NSHS applies to the development of border security strategy through its goal of preventing and disrupting terrorist attacks. One measure under that goal is to "deny terrorists, their weapons, and other terror-related materials entry to the homeland" (*National Strategy for Homeland Security* 2007, 15-16). This measure is approached in two parts. The first, prevention of terrorists from using legitimate pathways to enter the US. The second, prevention of terrorists from use of illicit pathways into the US (*National Strategy for Homeland Security* 2007, 18).

This second approach specifies the use of the Secure Border Initiative (SBI), an integration of people, technology, and tactical infrastructure, to detect, identify, respond to, and resolve illegal entry attempts at land borders. Tactical infrastructure is the portion of this approach that border barriers fall into. This approach also specifies the enhancement of current surveillance and the establishment of cooperation from bordering nations. (*National Strategy for Homeland Security* 2007, 18-19). The document also discusses the formulation of further strategy by using a risk management approach to focus limited security resources (*National Strategy for Homeland Security* 2007, 41).

Because the CBP and USBP strategies were published prior to The 2002 National Strategy for Homeland Security was also reviewed. This NSHS also does not specifically mention the use of border fencing. However, this version of the document does provide a section, labeled as a critical mission area, titled border and transportation security. This section emphasizes the improvement of border security by creating "smart borders" to allow effective non-intrusive screening of entering and exiting cargo and people. The only mention of preventing entry between POE's is written as "It [DHS] would monitor all our borders in order to detect illegal intrusions and intercept and apprehend smuggled goods and people attempting to enter illegally" (*National Strategy for Homeland Security* 2002, 22). This version of the NSHS also emphasizes the use of a risk management approach to allocate resources, stating "only allocate resources where the benefit of reducing risk is worth the amount of additional cost" (*National Strategy for Homeland Security* 2002, 64). Unlike the 2007 NSHS, this version provides specific priorities for the future. Of applicability to border security, the document lists the securing of America's borders by expanding the number of inspectors at POEs, purchasing additional inspection equipment, and testing and designing a system to track entry and exit of visitors. Creating "smart borders" is also listed as a priority. Under this priority use of risk management systems, biometric identification data, and partnerships with commercial organizations to pre-clear screened goods are listed (*National Strategy for Homeland Security* 2002, 68).

In January 2006 the CBP published *U.S. Customs and Border Protection 2005-2010 Strategic Plan*. This document outlines CBP's strategic goals and uses a military style of crosswalk to show how those goals and their associated objectives tie to DHS strategic goals (US Customs and Border Protection 2005, 14-17). It identifies the threat to the homeland as Al Qaeda and affiliated extremist groups (US Customs and Border Protection 2005, 9). The document also states the priority mission of the CBP is "to detect and prevent terrorists and terrorist weapons from entering the United States" (US Customs and Border Protection 2005, 6). The second strategic goal outlined is the preventing of terrorism between ports of entry. The first objective is to use intelligence driven operations to deploy its resources effectively against targets of greatest risk. The second objective is to maximize border security through the proper mix of personnel and capabilities along the northern, southern, and coastal borders. Under this objective the CBP states it will focus efforts on the southern and northern border similarly with the use of technology, checkpoints, and intelligence driven operations. The two borders differ in strategy by the CBP emphasis on establishing partnerships with Canadian law enforcement and intelligence while emphasizing the denial of access to urban areas, infrastructure, and routes of egress in the South. The third objective is to expand the training and capabilities of its specialized tactical units to rapidly respond to specific terrorist threats. The fourth objective is to develop a nationally directed program to ensure the training of personnel in the skills required to operate new technologies and to address infrastructure and facility needs (US Customs and Border Protection 2005, 23-26).

The USBP published its latest strategy in 2004. Although published prior to the CBP Strategic Plan, the USBP's National Border Patrol Strategy basically mirrors CBP's document in planned objectives and methods to achieve those objectives. The document addresses several issues with enforcement on the US-Mexico border. Specifically it acknowledges the increase in illegal immigrant deaths crossing in more remote areas, and that some would classify the majority of illegal aliens as "economic migrants. However, it states that there is an ever present threat that terrorists might use the same support systems as the illegal alien and attempt to use those aliens as cover to penetrate the border. To substantiate that threat the document further states that the USBP annually arrests aliens from "special interest" countries that, according to the State Department, pose a threat to the US (US Border Patrol 2004, 5-6).

In reference to the US-Canada border the USBP states several factors that make that border a security issue. The USBP recognizes that over ninety percent of Canada's population lives within one hundred miles of the border, and the presence of well-organized smuggling operations along the border. Additionally, the USBP states that although they have increased the number of agents on the US-Canada border, the "ability to detect, respond to, and interdict illegal cross-border penetrations along the US-Canada border remains limited". In order to adequately address the situation the USBP states that it must deploy more sensing and monitoring platforms on the US-Canada border (US Border Patrol 2004, 6).

This past year the CBP started the publication of a bi-annual magazine. Two articles in the Spring 2008 edition provide some key insight into CBP's understanding of the terrorist threat and its role in preventing or deterring that threat. David V. Aguilar, head of the CBP Office of Border Patrol, wrote an article discussing the securing of the US-Mexico border. In that article Chief Aguilar acknowledges that the stronger the USBP's enforcement presence has become the more dependent the illegal alien has become of smugglers. He further states, "Ironically the fact that more smuggling activity is occurring and the organizations are becoming more sophisticated can be seen as a measure of the impact our enforcement operations are having". According to Chief Aguilar the high level of illegal immigrant activity on the US-Mexico border decreases the amount of time those agents could be focusing on counter-terrorism and counter-narcotic operations. To substantiate this claim he cites the seventy-nine percent increase in the seizure of narcotics in the Rio Grande Valley sector when that same sector saw a decrease of thirty-four percent in overall illegal immigrants arrested and a sixty percent decrease in OTMs arrested. Chief Aguilar additionally cites the FY2007 twenty percent decrease in apprehensions, building of more than seventy miles of fence and addition of 2,500 agents as signs of progress on the US-Mexico border (Aguilar 2008).

Linda Kane, a staff writer for *Frontline* magazine, provides an overview of border enforcement along the US-Canada border. She acknowledges Ahmed Ressam's attempt to cross the border and the recent arrests seventeen terrorist suspects in Toronto, Canada, but states that most security risks to the US from Canada are from drug smuggling. She states that approximately thirty-three percent of Canada's gross domestic product depends upon trade with the US. The economic dependence between the US and Canada means that CBP officers must deal with the screening of a large quantity of goods at POEs. She uses a quote from Leslie Lawson, acting deputy division chief of the Operations Planning Analysis Division of the CBP Border Patrol to compare the security environments along the southern and northern borders. Lawson analogizes looking for terrorists on the southern border is like looking for a needle in a haystack and looking for a terrorist on the northern border is like looking for a contact lens in Yankee Stadium. The idea being that a terrorist can hide amongst illegal immigrants in the South while in the North a terrorist is hiding amongst the vastness of the border. Finally, she states that securing the border is a matter of finding a balance between resources, technology, and infrastructure, along with security cooperation with Canada (Kane 2008).

US immigration policy is another factor in securing the US borders against terrorism. In 2006 the Congressional Budget Office (CBO) published a report on US immigration policy. The report provides a good overview of the history of US immigration policy. It discusses how the Quota Law in 1921 established quotas by nationality based upon its representation in past census figures and how the Immigration and Nationality Act Amendments of 1965 abolished parts of that quota system. According to the report, the amendments focused legal immigration on the reunification of relatives and individuals with job skills within a preference system. While it did abolish caps on immigration from some countries it did not abolish caps for immigration for Eastern Hemisphere countries by preference category. The most recent immigration legislation, the Illegal Immigration Reform and Immigrant Responsibility Act of 1996

(IIRIRA), increased the numbers of USBP agents and reduced government benefits to illegal aliens. The Act also increased fines and punishments for certain convicted illegal immigrants and established a pilot program for verifying eligibility for immigrants applying for work and social services. The report also detailed immigrant categories and the enforcement of immigration laws under current policy (US Congress, Congressional Budget Office 2006).

The attempt to pass new immigration legislation was met with nation-wide protest and ultimately resulted in the failure of bills in the House and Senate. A Reuter's article in April 2006 reports on the numerous planned demonstrations in ninety-four towns and cities within the US (Jacobs 2006). In June of 2007 Rasmussen Reports posted an article providing analysis into why the 2007 immigration bill failed to pass. The article argues that the bill ultimately failed because the public did not perceive the bill would reduce illegal immigration, until the government enforces the border, the public will not be open to new immigration legislation (Rasmussen Reports 2007).

Methodology

Just as a vast review of literature is required in order to adequately understand the terrorist threat, border security, and US policy and strategy to counter that threat, an understanding of multiple methods of analysis is required to determine the appropriate method. In *Qualitative Data Anaylsis*, Miles and Huberman define qualitative analysis as the concurrent activities of data reduction, data display, and conclusion drawing and verification of data consisting of words instead of numbers (Miles and Huberman 1984, 21). The process of analysis involves reducing the data by selecting those portions of the raw data important to further analysis, then displaying that data into categories for analysis, and finally drawing conclusions from that display of data (Miles and Huberman 1984, 21-23). This process is interconnected and each part ongoing throughout the analysis, each activity may require further activity in another (Miles and Huberman 1984, 23).

In *Qualitative Evaluations and Research Methods*, Patton provides key insight into the differences between description and interpretation. He states that the description portion of qualitative analysis provides a reader with "sufficient description to allow the reader to understand the basis for an interpretation", and "in such a way that others reading the results can understand and draw their own interpretations" (Patton 1990, 430, 375). He further elaborates on description by stating that analysis makes the description manageable and leads to interpretation. This is a fine balance in that "description must not be so 'thin' as to remove context or meaning" (Patton 1990, 430). Interpretation will "identify significant patterns and construct a frame work for communicating the essence of what the data reveal" (Patton 1990, 371-372). He states that readers will make their own judgments regardless of the interpretation by the analyst, but those "opinions and speculations...deserve to be reported" (Patton 1990, 431).

Empirical Political Analysis provides explanations of both quantitative and qualitative analysis for use in the research of areas within the political science field. In regards to "comparative research", it states that this approach "allows us to generalize beyond the sometimes narrow confine of a single culture and ... permits us to test for the effects of system-wide characteristics" (Manheim, Rich, Willnat, and Brians 2008, 214). Selection of questions that apply cross-culturally is important to the validity of this comparison. Identical variables can be used as long as they mean the same thing in every

country in the study (Manheim, Rich, Willnat, and Brians 2008, 215-217).

CHAPTER 3

RESEARCH METHODOLOGY

Introduction

The goal of counter-terrorism is to prevent a terrorist attack. Legislation, presidential directives, and strategic documents, specify that the securing of US borders is a requirement to effectively counter a terrorist attack. The proposed building of a border fence is one means that the US government has determined as an option that achieves or fulfills a requirement to achieve a secure border. This study attempts to determine how the US-Mexico border fence, as constructed and as a matter of policy, effects a terrorist's ability to gain entrance into the US. By determining how well the US-Mexico border fence supports the US counter-terrorism strategy, this study contributes to the anti-terrorism literature.

Research Design

The research design encompasses the qualitative analysis subsets of descriptive, interpretive, and comparative approaches to determine the efficacy of building a border fence to deter or defeat a terrorist attack within the US. Each approach is necessary to break down the complex relationship between border security and counter-terrorism, and to obtain a holistic understanding of the problem. Each approach will be used to define the land based terrorist threat, and analyze how US border security has met that threat. To do this one must first understand who the terrorist is and the methods in which that terrorist operates. The US has two land borders, one north and one south. Because the Mexican border has fenced portions while the Canadian border generally does not, it allows comparison between fenced and unfenced border on the same case – the United

States. It also allows comparison between human flows as influenced by policies and

procedures unrelated to physical barriers. Finally an examination is conducted of US

policies and their independent effect on countering terrorist activity. Analysis of the

results from each subject sequentially will provide the necessary information to form

conclusions as to the efficacy of a US-Mexico border fence as a counter-terrorism

measure.

Descriptive analysis will organize the data to provide the reader with "sufficient

description to allow the reader to understand the basis for an interpretation", and "in such

a way that others reading the results can understand and draw their own interpretations"

(Patton 1990, 430, 375). It will provide evidence of terrorist methods used to gain

territorial access and the requirements to support past terrorist attacks. Because no

terrorist has gained territorial access to the US via the US-Mexico border, evidence of

methods of entry by illegal aliens will be analyzed as possible methods for terrorists to

gain access. Also investigations simulating terrorist attempts to cross the US-Mexico and

US-Canada border will be used in this analysis. Descriptive analysis will also provide an

understanding of past and current border security legislation, policy, strategy, procedures,

and operations, and how current perceptions among the populace and governing officials

have formed. This understanding also applies to the US land bordering nations of

Canada and Mexico.

Interpretation will "identify significant patterns and construct a framework for

communicating the essence of what the data reveal" (Patton 1990, 371-372). Interpretive

analysis will be used to establish an understanding of the methods that a terrorist would use to gain entrance into the US, and other border traversing requirements for a terrorist to conduct an attack. By determining each method and requirement, and subsequently analyzing the bordering nations' and the border fence's effect on those methods and requirements, one can obtain an understanding of how and to what extent a border fence deters or defeats terrorism. The "Al Qaeda Manual" will be the base document for determining the terrorist requirements for using a bordering nation as a transit into the US. Interpretive analysis will also be used to determine patterns and connections that currently influence the building of a border fence.

The comparative analysis, comparing and contrasting the differences and similarities between the US-Mexico and US-Canada borders will be conducted to find reasons for the historically different record of attempted terrorist crossings. By using identical variables, obtained through the analysis of the terrorist threat, that apply for both regions valid results can be obtained (Manheim, Rich, Willnat, and Brians 2008, 214-218). This analysis will provide the majority of the data for determining recommendations for the future counter-terrorism strategy along the US borders. The comparative analysis will compare current surveillance and manning of the two borders and the bi-national cooperative strategy conducted on the two borders. Most importantly the cultural, governmental policy and demographic differences between Canada and Mexico will be analyzed to obtain additional understanding in regards to which culture better supports the terrorist requirements for conducting a surreptitious crossing of the US border.

CHAPTER 4

ANALYSIS

Introduction

In order to analyze the whole issue of border security and the efficacy of a border

fence, the data collected is analyzed according to its category and in a sequence to

provide a complete understanding of the entire problem. This is first done by defining

the threat and its method of operation. Second, analysis is done of the two potential host

countries to determine the ability of those regions to support the threat as defined in the

first analysis. Third, the state of border security is analyzed to determine what effects

border security and border fencing would have against a terrorist. Finally, analysis is

conducted on US border security policy and strategy to determine how they address both

the threat and the current state of border security.

Terrorist Requirements

The latest National Intelligence Estimate for Homeland Security, the 2004 Rand

Corporation terrorist assessment, and all strategic documents related to homeland security

state that Al Qaeda is the most serious threat to homeland security. The concurrence of

these documents validates the use of Al Qaeda as the most salient threat to homeland

security. Consequently, an understanding as to how Al Qaeda or an Al Qaeda inspired

terrorist organization operates must be obtained to evaluate the effectiveness of current

border security strategy.

While Al Qaeda doesn't publish doctrine readily available for the public, the

seized Al Qaeda manual fills this void. The Rand study also used the Al Qaeda manual to determine some of the operational requirements of a terrorist organization (Cragin and Daly 2004, 48). Individual and organizational requirements as listed in the Al Qaeda training manual are listed in the figure below. By focusing on those requirements most necessary to the successful surreptitious crossing of the US land border, we glean several requirements from the Al Qaeda training manual. Those requirements are the individual qualification of a member to be of the Islamic faith, and the organizational requirements of forged documents, transportation, and apartments and hiding places.

Individual Requirements and Characteristics

1. **Islam**
2. Commitment to the Organization's Ideology
3. Maturity
4. Sacrifice
5. Listening and Obedience
6. Keeping Secrets and Concealing Information
7. Free of Illness
8. Patience
9. Tranquility and "Unflappability"
10. Intelligence and Insight
11. Caution and Prudence
12. Truthfulness and Counsel
13. Ability to Observe and Analyze
14. Ability to Act, Change Positions, and Conceal Oneself

Military Organizational Requirements

1. **Forged documents and counterfeit currency**
2. **Apartments and hiding places**
3. Communication means
4. **Transportation means**
5. Information
6. Arms and ammunition
7. Transport [of arms and ammunition]

Figure 4.   Military Organizational Requirements
Source: Created by Author, information from *Al Qaeda Manual* n.d., 12.

The Al Qaeda training manual lists the first qualification of a member is to be of the Muslim faith, stating that a person who does not believe in Islam is incapable of defending the goals and secrets of the organization (Al Qaeda Manual n.d., 15). Any terrorist attempting to transit into the US from a bordering nation would require some level of logistical support. From this requirement it is logical that an Al Qaeda operative would perceive the need or, minimally, the preference to use other Muslims for support in order to maintain operational security. Additionally, a terrorist organization could attempt to recruit operatives from the bordering nation. Given the common occurrence and high frequency of travel of citizens from Mexico and Canada, one could argue that recruitment of operatives from either nation would be preferable. The Al Qaeda Manual lists smugglers and those seeking political asylum as candidates for recruitment (Al Qaeda Manual n.d., 93). In essence, terrorists and potential supporters must plausibly be of the Muslim faith, and so committed to the cause that they would be willing to "undergo martyrdom" (Al Qaeda Manual n.d., 15).

Another requirement of operational security is the use of identification documents. While the US entrance scenario discussed in this paper involves a terrorist crossing between POEs, a terrorist would most likely require identification documents at some point in their travel. The Al Qaeda training manual specifically discusses the use of false identification documents (Al Qaeda Manual n.d., 22-23). The document requirement would occur either upon entrance to that transit nation or entrance at a nation bordering that transit nation. However, it could be argued that personal identification would not be required if the terrorist gained entrance to that bordering nation surreptitiously. Two of the millennium bombing suspects illegally disembarked an

Algerian ship as stowaways when it landed at the Norfolk port (Malkin 2002, 6). However, a terrorist may find US identification necessary to continue operating within the US. Abdelghani Meskini, one of the two stowaways, rented a vehicle and flew on commercial aircraft, both of which would require personal identification (Bernton, Carter, Heath, and Neff 2002, Chapter 14).

One critical requirement to a surreptitious crossing of the US land border would be transportation. Whether the terrorist planned to cross the border on foot or using a vehicle, transportation would be required to reach the crossing point. In reference to transportation, the manual approves the use of public and private transportation, and discusses security measures in their use (Al Qaeda Manual n.d., 39-42). It does not discuss the use of transportation for crossing borders.

Regardless, in order to obtain transportation support, the terrorist would additionally require a base from which to operate. This requirement is portrayed in the fiction Pandora's Legion (Coyle and Tillman 2007, 293-294). Throughout the Al Qaeda training manual and specifically in reference to base locations, transportation, and general movement, it continually stresses the need to blend in with the environment and the local populace. The requirement to blend in could logically be determined as an additional need for the terrorist attempting to surreptitiously cross the US border.

The US government has stated and terrorism analysis supports that Al Qaeda is the primary threat capable of conducting an attack against the US homeland. Historically, Al Qaeda or Al Qaeda type terrorists, Sunni jihadists, have gained entrance into the US by manipulating the US immigration system. Forty of the forty-six documented cases of terrorists that have entered the US, entered the US legally and only eleven of those forty remained illegally or violated US immigration law (see Appendix A). This fact does not negate the possibility that a terrorist could attempt to cross the US land border surreptitiously, if conditions warranted that approach. This means the type of terrorist of greatest concern that would attempt a surreptitious crossing of the US land border would most likely operate in a manner consistent with Al Qaeda doctrine. That doctrine requires an operative to be of the Islamic faith; consequently Al Qaeda would most likely choose to cross a border from a host country that could supply a Muslim population base to provide the support necessary to assist a crossing. Not only would that location provide supporters, but potentially could provide the operative himself, who would be able to blend in with the populace. Additionally, the operative would find that a location that provided accessibility to false identification documents and transportation favorable to increasing his likelihood of success.

Myth of the Mexican Menace

Since the days of Pancho Villa and his bands of raiders crossing into the American southwest, the US-Mexico border has conjured up images of lawlessness and danger. It is true that violence has once again increased along the border, but much of it is a result of Mexico's effort to reform and rid itself of drug traffickers, and the huge amounts of capital infused into those criminal elements by American buyers. Prior to the 1980's, drug trafficking of cocaine into the United States ran primarily through the Caribbean. Once the US war on drugs began to squeeze drug trafficking out of the Caribbean, Columbian drug manufacturers began to look for a new route into the US. The ungoverned US-Mexico border and Mexico's large pool of unemployed citizens provided a prime opportunity for re-establishing their illegal trade (Payan 2006, 25-28).

These Mexican drug traffickers are now fighting over a leadership vacuum imposed by the imprisonment of many of their past leaders (Mexican Trucker Online, entry posted June 2, 2008). The US Ambassador Antonio O. Garza has stated that the drug cartels in Mexico "have crossed a line from endangering bystanders … to intentionally targeting civilians" (Carl 2008). Ironically, much of the violence in Mexico is supported by the trafficking of weapons from the US into Mexico (Border Security Conference 2008).

Like the demand for drugs, the US demand for cheap labor provides another pull for illegal activity along the US-Mexico border. This demand is fueled by Mexico's under-educated and under-employed workforce and the US's increasingly educated workforce (Hanson 2007, 14). Increased law enforcement along the border to stop illegal immigration has had a similar effect as that of law enforcement to stop drug smuggling. Without another viable option, law enforcement has increased the dependence of the illegal immigrant on human smugglers to cross the border and has pushed that immigration to less enforced areas. This increase in dependence has in turn provided the capital to the coyote to buy better capabilities (Payan 2006, 59, 69-71), which could be exploited by terrorists seeking entry to the US.

It would be misleading not to mention the fact that OTMs (Other Than Mexican) illegal immigrants are crossing the border. Congressman Tom Tancredo has stated that USBP records indicate the apprehension of 132 nationals from countries considered a security threat since 2001. A smuggling route along the Arizona border with Mexico has even earned the local name of the "Arab Road" (Fox News 2005). Also a market for smuggling in OTMs has been established as evidenced in Tony Payan's account of his encounter with a coyote in Mexico. He details in his book *The Three U.S.-Mexico*

Border Wars his approach of a coyote who quoted him prices of $6,000 to smuggle a Cuban and $1,000 to smuggle a Middle-Easterner (Payan 2006, 69). However, it would be false to assume that just because an illegal immigrant is Muslim or of another ethnic background than Mexican that they are a terrorist. Many of the Arab countries in the world have economies just as impoverished as Mexico's. With an increased reluctance by the US to grant visas for those countries, it could be argued that those individuals who are looking for work are given a new incentive for illegally crossing the border by land.

Although the assumption that someone of Arab descent or of the Muslim faith is a terrorist is unjustified at best, one could argue that the larger the group of people of this type, the greater the possibility an Islamic terrorist could find some type of support. Mexico's Muslim population is very small, believed to be only a couple thousand (Zambellis 2006). Comparatively, the US Muslim population makes up 0.6 percent of its total population or approximately two million Muslims (CIA World Fact Book 2008). Although most Mexican Muslims immigrated at the later part of the Ottoman rule, there has been a recent increase in new converts in the Chiapas region of Mexico (Zambellis 2006). This region is also home to the Zapatista rebels. Spanish Muslims did make an ideological pact with these rebels in the 1990s. However, that pact was primarily attributable to their more fundamental Islamic values that were contrary to the capitalist use of usury than any political motivation (Glüsing 2005).

The fact that most of the Muslims that have immigrated to Mexico did so many years ago, along with their small size, is representative of Mexico's strict immigration laws. However, taking account of the increase of illegal immigrants from other Latin American countries entering the US via Mexico, it is unclear how strictly these laws are enforced. Neither is it clear if transiting Mexico is considered illegal immigration by the Mexican government.

The lack of a large Muslim population and strict immigration laws is not to say that Mexico has not encountered terrorism. In fact, violence in Mexico has been on the rise. The grenade attack in Morelia set a new level of violence for the drug cartels through their targeting of civilians, sparking calls from the Mexican government for renewed resolve against the drug cartels and terrorism. But again, this is narco-terrorism, not Jihadist terrorism. Mexico has also had instances of international terrorist organizations operating within their borders. The FARC (Revolutionary Armed Forces of Columbia) did have an office at the National Autonomous University of Mexico, but that was closed by the Mexican government in 2002 (Lange 2008). The ETA (Fatherland and Liberty), a Basque separatist terrorist group, also had a presence in Mexico prior to the 1990's when Mexico agreed to no longer treat suspected ETA members as political refugees, and signed an extradition agreement with Spain (BBC Online 2004). None of these organizations, at present, are a direct threat to the US via cross-border attacks. Additionally, Mexico has agreed to all anti-terrorism measure requests by the US government following the 9/11 terrorist attacks and has participated in anti-terrorism exercises with the US.

It is important to consider the ease with which illegal immigrants have entered the US via Mexico, and Mexico's current struggle to contain narco-violence. It is also important to recognize Mexico's cooperation with the US in counter-terrorist operations along with the fact that their immigration laws and policies have inhibited the establishment of a significant Muslim population. The fact still remains that there has been no documented case of a terrorist gaining entrance into the US from Mexico. We must assume that terrorists are intelligent and will seek the means to enter the US that provides them with the most likelihood of success. The question remains as to why they haven't used Mexico for that purpose. It could be that Mexico doesn't naturally provide them with the support requirements to successfully gain entrance into the US. However, that may change as coyotes gain capabilities. Without a viable option for the illegal immigrant, a coyote can name his price and use that profit to enhance his capabilities. It may be that our policy of enforcement against illegal immigration creates an increasing market for the coyote. That increasing market in turn could provide him with the capital necessary to gain the means to transport terrorists across the border, and also provide the cover for the terrorist to blend in with the populous.

The harshness of the environment on the US-Mexico border may be one other reason why terrorists have not chosen that border as a means of infiltrating into the US. The area now favored by illegal immigrants is the Tucson Sector in Arizona. Although USBP presence in that sector has greatly increased in the past ten years, its remoteness and harsh landscape make it that much more difficult to enforce. The environment also makes it more difficult to survive, especially on foot. In a November 12, 2008 broadcast of "National Geographic Explorer" titled *Border Wars*, the area was named the devil's highway because of the number of people who have disappeared and presumably died in the arid desert of the Tucson Sector. So many remains have been recovered that a forensic scientist had to be hired full time and a new facility had to be built in the town of Tucson to store and record all the recovered remains. Additionally, the program reported that in the middle of the summer the three day walk from the border to Tucson requires

62

fifty pounds of water for the average male (National Geographic Explorer, originally aired on the National Geographic Channel, November 12, 2008).

While there has been an increase in violence in Mexico it provides more of an indicator of the Mexican government's commitment to rid itself of corruption rather than a threat to the US homeland. Unfortunately these efforts are primarily focused against the drug cartels. While these efforts could have some effect against human trafficking, the Mexican government has not taken direct action against the coyotes. Additionally, the increased enforcement along the border has increased the dependence of illegal immigrants on coyotes and the cost of that assistance. With new capital to finance increased capabilities the coyotes could have the capability to transport a terrorist across the US-Mexico border and provide the identification documents necessary for further operation within the US.

Mexico has a very small Muslim population, a condition not likely to change considering Mexico's immigration policies. Such a small Muslim population would require Al Qaeda to take additional risk by enlisting the cooperation of non-Muslims and inhibiting the ability to blend in with or recruit from the populace. The increase in US law enforcement on the border has also pushed illegal immigration, and consequently a terrorist, to more remote and dangerous areas. Considering the extreme environmental conditions and lack of Muslim population, it makes sense that terrorists have historically chosen a more hospitable and less enforced region. This effect, though, may be fleeting as coyotes adapt to US law enforcement. Unless measures are taken to stop the financing of coyotes, an Al Qaeda terrorist may choose the US-Mexico border as a possible option for entrance into the US in the future. However, if more favorable conditions were available in another location or by another means, it is unlikely that Al Qaeda would choose to use the US-Mexico border regardless of the capability of the coyotes.

The Canadian Conundrum

The US populace commonly views Canada as a friendly northern neighbor, practically another part of the US. This view is reinforced by the two countries' common origins as colonies of Great Britain, although their attainment of sovereignty from Great Britain took distinctly different paths. Additionally, the US has enjoyed a prolonged period of peaceful relations with Canada and shared military alliances. The last conflict with the region now known as Canada was during the War of 1812, almost one hundred years prior to the US Punitive Expedition into Mexico in 1916. With a common cultural origin and language, and a common need to populate vast expanses of land, it is easy to see why the US populace views Canada as a country much like their own.

Canada and the US have also shared similar policies on immigration. Early on, both countries depended upon an open immigration policy to facilitate the settlement of their large land areas. With most of these immigrants coming from Europe, both countries' policies changed little except in response to large influxes of immigrants from non-European areas. Like the US, Canada adopted new immigration laws in the 1920s to facilitate the immigration of only individuals of "desirable" race or ethnicity, primarily of European descent (Specific Events & Topics, Immigration Acts 1866-2001, Canada in the Making). The two nation's immigration laws were also similarly revised in the late 1960's to end discrimination against immigration based upon nationality and established preference systems for categories of immigrants. Both countries prioritized immigrants based upon occupational skills and immediate relatives, but unlike Canada, the US did not completely abolish caps on immigration for those from certain countries. Consequently, Canada received a large influx of non-European immigrants (US Congress, Congressional Budget Office 2006).

Another difference in immigration policy between Canada and the US is that of asylum or refugee status for immigrants. Canada provides a much more liberal approach to offering and determining asylum for immigrants and grants a higher percentage of applicants refugee status than the US (Smick 2006). Even if an individual in Canada is found residing illegally within the country that person is seldom deported. In reference to illegal immigration, the 2002 Director of Canada's intelligence agency stated "Once someone sets foot in Canada, then it is very hard and takes a very long time to get them out" (Bernton, Carter, Heath, and Neff 2002, Chapter 4).

Yet another difference in immigration policy is that the granting of legal immigration is somewhat decentralized in Canada. Provinces in Canada can determine who is granted legal immigration. The non-uniform policy further concentrates immigrants into destination cities that are less restrictive on immigration. With the Canadian populace already concentrated in a few metropolitan areas near the US border, the concentration of immigrants in these areas is compounded and further impedes their assimilation into Canadian society. Unassimilated communities may be more fertile for the development of support networks.

This concentration of immigrants includes a large Muslim population that has doubled in size in four out of five provinces in the last ten years under the liberalized Canadian immigration policies (Provincial and Territorial Highlights, Religions in Canada, Census of Canada 2001). As stated previously, it would be false to assume that

65

every individual or group of individuals of Islamic faith would support Islamic terrorists, but it is logical to assume that the larger the group the greater the possibility that Islamic extremist supporters are present within that group. This assumption is supported by the examples of Abu Mezer and Ahmed Ressam, the only documented terrorists who have entered the US at a POE or between POEs along the US land border.

Both Mezer and Ressam manipulated the liberal immigration policies of Canada and took advantage of Canada's history of non-enforcement of immigration law. This manipulation included the use of readily available fraudulent documents. Although both had been arrested for law violation prior to their final apprehension, they were repeatedly allowed to remain and travel within that country. In Ressam's case, to even travel to Afghanistan for training in an Al Qaeda camp.

The Canadian government has made some changes since these incidents with the passing of the Canadian Immigration and Refugee Act, 2001, and signing of security agreements with the US. The US and Canada have created Integrated Border Enforcement Teams to further the execution of complimentary operations and information exchange in relation to border security. Canada has also shutdown many Islamic charities suspected as being fronts for funneling money to terrorist organizations and banned groups such as Hezbollah and Hamas from operating within Canada (Anti-Defamation League 2004). However, the Islamic extremist activity still continues within Canada and liberal immigration policies still pose a problem.

The arrest of seventeen Al Qaeda inspired suspected terrorists in Toronto in 2006 (Associated Press 2006), exemplifies the continuing problem of the inability to assimilate some portions of Canada's large Muslim population. The fact that all of the suspects

66

were either Canadian citizens or legal residents of Canada does not negate the example and could be reflective of another terrorist threat issue, the radicalization of Muslim citizens of developed countries. Regardless, the tracking of immigration violators in Canada remains an issue. While the numbers of illegal aliens residing in Canada does not reach the numbers in the US, it is estimated that there are between 100,000 and 200,000 undocumented immigrants in Canada. Many are failed refugee applicants that never left the country and few of these, if pursued, are deported after apprehension (Smick 2006).

The type of terrorist threat that could come from Canada was tested in a GAO investigation in 2007. The investigators found that "a determined cross-border violator would likely be able to bring radioactive materials or other contraband undetected in the United States by crossing the US-Canada border at any of the locations we investigated" (US Government Accountability Office, Kutz 2007, 12). Even the USBP has stated that the "ability to detect, respond to, and interdict illegal cross-border penetrations along the US-Canada border remains limited" (US Border Patrol 2004, 6).

Finally, the geographic character of the US-Canada border poses another challenge to border security. This border is nearly twice the length of the US-Mexico border of 1,952 miles. The vegetation along the border also makes detection of illegal crossers problematic. One of the county sheriffs that border British Columbia stated "We have a lot of wilderness here, and you're lucky if you can see 30 feet" (Egan 1997). Obviously it would take an enormous number of border patrol officers to adequately cover such a length, especially without a border fence or some type of barrier in place to slow down a would be crosser.

There are some natural water barriers and the severe winters could deter would be crossers. Abu Mezer and his crossing accomplice did show signs of hypothermia the first time Mezer was apprehended (US Department of Justice 1998, sec. II D 2.b.i.). However, these winters also provide a bridge for illegal crossers as many border waterways sufficiently freeze to allow travel by foot or vehicle, and can ice communication towers. The northern border region also provides "thousands of potential accessible routes into the US" (Kane 2008). As demonstrated by the GAO study, the investigators could have just as easily crossed in to the US from Canada using a vehicle as they had done by walking.

Canada's similar, though more liberal, immigration policy has facilitated not only an increasingly large Muslim population, but one that is concentrated in a few urban areas. The two major concentrations of Muslims have occurred in Toronto and Montreal, the areas which Abu Mezer and Ahmed Ressam immigrated to respectively. As demonstrated by these two terrorists and other terrorist events, these areas not only have the ability to provide a base of support, cover for blending in, and fraudulent documents, it has also provided a pool for terrorist recruitment. While the harsh winters in this border region could provide some deterrent, it also could provide additional means of access to a well outfitted terrorist. The risk created by exposure to that environment is also counterbalanced by the GAO's finding of numerous paved roads in proximity of the border and lack of detection when simulating illegal crossings. Additionally, the harsh winter environment also challenges the use of technology there, and creates additional crossing opportunities by freezing natural water barriers. The US-Canada border appears to provide more opportunity for a successful crossing by an Al Qaeda or Al Qaeda recruited terrorist than does the US-Mexico border.

Effects of the Fence

Determining what effects the US-Mexico border fence as constructed today or as prescribed in legislation and national security strategy will have against a terrorist is fraught with snares of political bias and oversimplification of cause and effect. To date, there is no recorded event of a terrorist being defeated or deterred by the fence. There is no terrorist who has described a border barrier thwarting his attempt to cross the US land border, nor its presence influencing his attempt. In fact, there is no documented attempt or threat to attempt a crossing of the US-Mexico land border by a terrorist. Lacking this hard evidence, the substitute of an actual terrorist attempt with a simulation of a terrorist attempting to cross the land border or an illegal immigrant attempting the crossing provides the best means to determine the effect of a border fence on a terrorist.

In the case of a simulated terrorist attempting a crossing, the GAO's 2007 study is the only publically available document of testing of border security between POEs. Unfortunately, the GAO investigating agents found it too much of a safety risk to approach the US-Mexico border from the Mexican side.

The reaction of the USBP to the actions of the investigators at the preliminary site might seem understandable, considering the fact that walking up to an international border is not criminal nor necessarily suspicious in and of itself. However, taking into account that no other public traffic occurred for the entire hour the investigators were in the area, the investigators' activity could have seemed suspicious (US Government Accountability Office, Kutz 2007, 8). Additionally, it is conceivable that a terrorist or illegal alien would use the support of someone already across the border to facilitate their crossing. More importantly however, is to remember the fact that the smuggling of weapons from the US into Mexico is already a major problem, demonstrating an evolving real threat on US borders (Border Security Conference 2008). Achieving USBP's strategic goal to "gain, maintain, and expand operational control" of the border would require not only controlling the entrance of people and equipment, but their exit as well (US Border Patrol 2004, 9).

Although the pedestrian fence was not tested and investigators did not approach the border from the Mexican side in the GAO study, important conclusions may be drawn as far as the effects of the fence. The investigators, acting as potential terrorists, did avoid areas that had visible law enforcement presence and areas that were fenced against foot traffic. Apparently the fence would have a turning or diverting effect on a terrorist and that could be construed as a deterrent effect. However, when investigators were within visual surveillance of USBP agents, their activity did not elicit a response. This in turn raises questions as to USBP agents' understanding of the current threat environment.

CRS has provided a study of border barriers and has continually updated that study, as recently as May of 2008. As the San Diego Fence is the longest standing border barrier, it is the focus of the portion of the study dedicated to evaluating the effectiveness of border fencing. Another USBP sector along the US-Mexico border is the Tucson Sector (see figure 5). The Tucson sector at the time of the study was not fenced, and consequently was included in the study to compare it to the San Diego Sector. While there are other non-fenced sectors that could have been chosen for comparison, it appears that the Tucson Sector was chosen because it provided a more notable change in numbers of apprehensions in comparison to the decreases in the San Diego Sector.

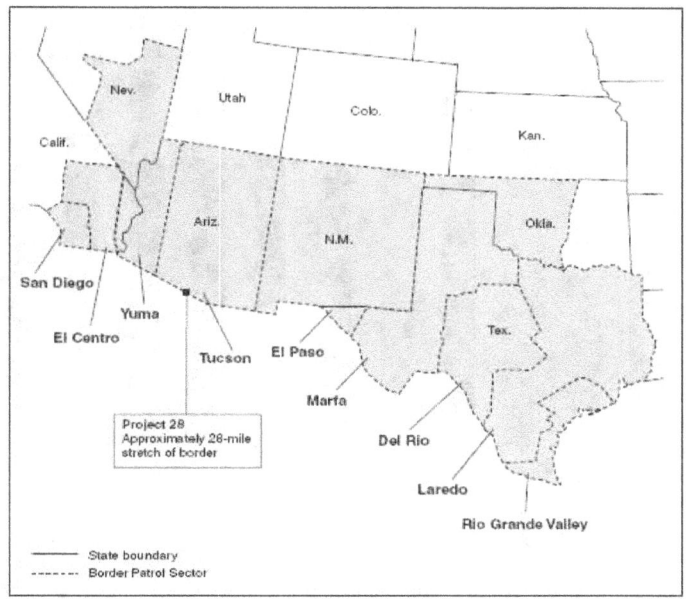

Figure 5.   Map of Border Patrol Sectors Along the Southwest Border
Source: US Government Accountability Office, SECURE BORDER INITIATIVE, *Observations on the Importance of Applying Lessons Learned to Future Projects* (Location: GAO, February 27, 2008), 5

Using the graphed apprehension data provided by the CRS report, the author added important enforcement events also detailed in that report (see figure 6). Because the San Diego fence was constructed in stages and as one part of the increased enforcement effort in the San Diego sector, it is necessary to also consider the increase in agents deployed to that sector. The addition of these events provides a better understanding of the whole enforcement effort in relation to the numbers of apprehensions.

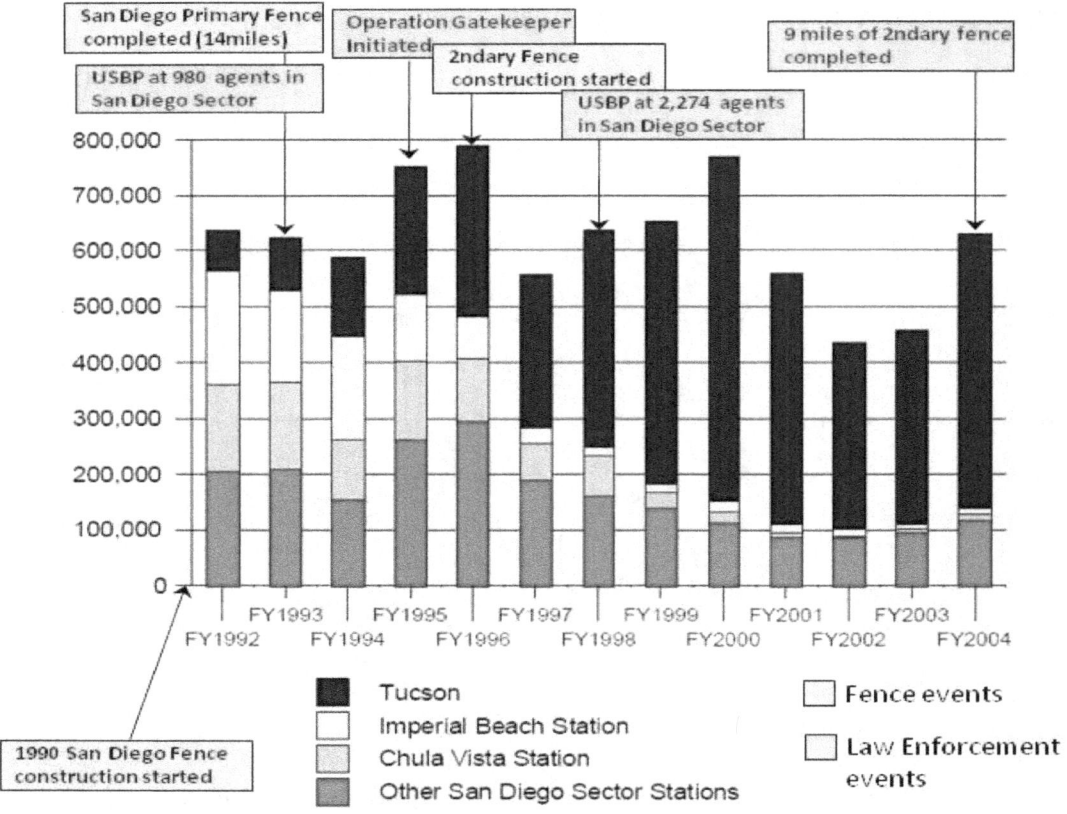

Figure 6. Apprehensions at San Diego Sector Stations and Tucson Sector
Source: CRS analysis of CBP data, Border Security: Barriers Along the U.S.
International Border (Location: CRS, March 21, 2008), 17, Author added event
information.

This graphic depiction of apprehensions in the two sectors demonstrates that the

primary San Diego Fence had little deterrent effect on illegal immigration in the San

Diego sector as a whole. Once Operation Gatekeeper was initiated, apprehensions at the

Imperial Beach station drastically decreased, while apprehensions increased in other

stations and sectors. According to the CRS this appears to suggest a migration of illegal

immigration eastward, away from the areas of increased enforcement and fencing

(Library of Congress 2008, 17). It is also important to note that total apprehensions overall increased in FY1996, then decreased again in FY1997 after initiation of the secondary fence construction, but total apprehensions began increasing again. The one consistent trend is that apprehensions in the San Diego Sector continued to decrease over time. This seems to suggest that the increase in enforcement in the San Diego Sector had the most effect in decreasing apprehensions, but had little effect in total apprehensions for the Tucson and San Diego sectors as a whole. In fact, the USBP apprehensions for 1992 and 2004 were the same, 1.2 million total unauthorized aliens apprehended (Library of Congress 2008, 17). Illegal immigration had simply migrated to a new sector. It also seems to suggest that there is some other factor or factors that are affecting the increase and decrease in total numbers of apprehensions.

There are strong indications that the US economy has as much or more to do with the rate of illegal immigration into the US than immigration law enforcement. The body of literature suggest that most illegal immigrants migrate to the US in order to obtain employment or better wages than they could expect to obtain within their own country. Gonzalez suggests that the drop in illegal crossings is tied directly to the slowing US economy. The article cites research conducted by Dawn McLaren, a research economist at Arizona State University, that correlates increases in numbers of apprehensions to a strong US economy (Gonzalez 2007). Additionally, Tony Payan stated, "In regard to undocumented migration, even more than in illegal drugs, it is possible to say with certainty that it's economics" (Payan 2006, 65).

Generally, the performance of the US economy is measured by percent growth in Gross Domestic Product (GDP), from year to year. The Bureau of Economic Analysis (BEA), a bureau of the US Department of Commerce, is the primary authority and recorder of this data. Graphing the data provided by the BEA website for the percentage change from the previous economic quarter allows for the plotting of a yearly trend line that visually represents the performance of the US economy. In order to develop a representation of the economy that could be applied to the time period and fiscal years of apprehensions used in the CRS analysis, quarterly data from the fourth quarter of the previous year through the third quarter of that year was used to show fiscal years (FY). Additionally, data was collected from FY 1990 and 1991 to allow for a more accurate depiction of the trend line for FY 1992. This trend line, a four period moving average, depicts the year to year percentage growth in US GDP (see figure 7).

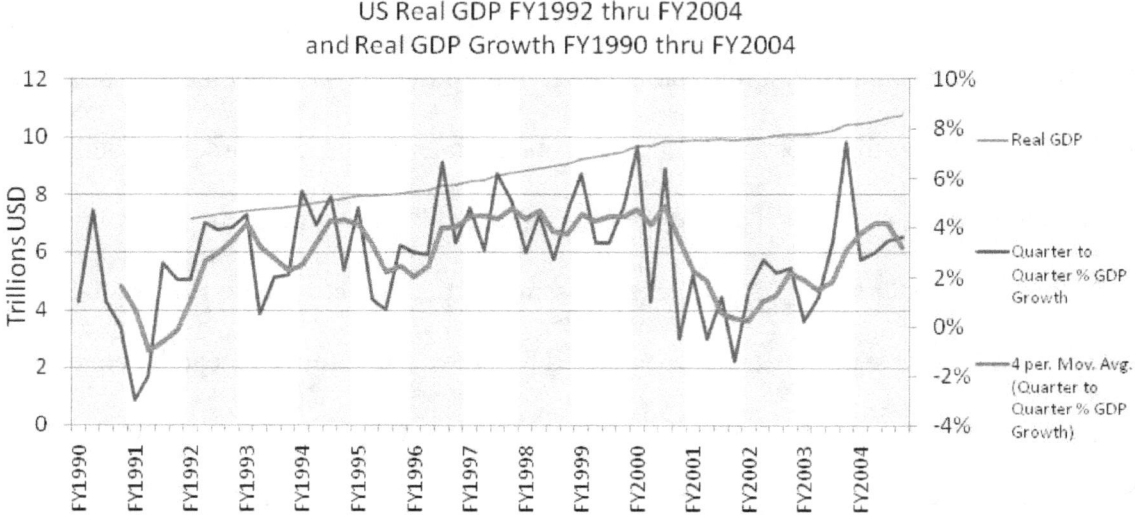

Figure 7.   US Real GDP for FY1992 through FY2004 and
Percentage GDP Growth for FY1990 through FY2004
Source: Author created, Data from BEA website

The US GDP graph shows a decrease in economic performance from the end of FY 1992 to FY 1994, a period in which total numbers of apprehensions also decreased (comparing figures 6 and 7). Additionally, as the US economy was in a period of prolonged growth from FY 1997 into FY 2000 apprehensions increased. During the 2001 recession and slow improvement of the US economy from FY 2002 to FY 2004 apprehension seem to match the general economic trend. While the trend of apprehensions does appear to generally correlate, there are a couple of fiscal years where US economic performance and numbers of apprehensions do not correlate.

An interesting anomaly occurs in FY 1997. In a period of prolonged economic growth figure 6 shows that total numbers of apprehensions greatly decreased. In late September of 1996 the Illegal Immigration Reform and Immigrant Responsibility Act of 1996 (IIRIRA) was signed into law. This change in policy and law may have been enough to deter, at least initially, illegal immigrants from crossing into the US from Mexico. It also may have been that it took a period of time for coyotes and other facilitators of illegal immigration to overcome the new security measures imposed by IIRIRA. All this suggests that economic conditions and employment policies have explanatory power on human flows independent of, and possibly greater than, physical barriers.

It is not the point of this paper to state that the economy is the sole cause of fluctuations in illegal immigration or an incentive for terrorist border crossings. However, it is apparent that the US economy is a major factor that influences the rate of illegal immigration and the ease with which terrorists could blend in with human flows. Over-simplification of cause and effect causes misdirected efforts in controlling the border and in the prevention of a possible surreptitious crossing of a terrorist between POEs. The US economy's influence on illegal immigration indicates that enforcement at the border alone cannot stop the flow of illegal immigration. A terrorist attempting to cross between POEs would most likely want to blend in with the populace as was previously noted in the Al Qaeda Manual. Continued illegal immigration provides a population in which a terrorist could hide and a human smuggling network to facilitate his infiltration.

It appears true that the fence, combined with increases in enforcement, have had a deterrent effect. This deterrent effect however, has been to move would-be illegal crossers to areas less visibly enforced. However, the turning effect that increased law enforcement and barriers have achieved is limited. The deterrence and logistical cost effects could be fleeting, as human smugglers adapt to the changing security environment. Dedicated terrorists would be less easy to deter than migrant workers.

Even where barriers have been placed along the US-Mexico border there are numerous instances of breaches. These breaches include building ramps over vehicle barriers, using ropes and climbing ladders to get over fences, digging under the fences, and even the construction of complex tunnels. In a recent broadcast of "National Geographic Explorer" titled *Border Wars* (aired November 12, 2008) one of the agents patrolling the San Diego fence told of the discovery of two such tunnels underneath the fence that connected Mexico to the US. One of these tunnels was eighty-five feet below the surface, a depth beyond the ability of ground penetrating radar to detect. Recently one of seven tunnels built in the last several years in the Calexico, California area was discovered (Marosi 2008), and another possible tunnel was discovered south of Yuma, Arizona (Gilbert, 2008).

Simulated border crossings and apprehension data appear to show that a terrorist would avoid an area with border fencing and visible surveillance, as has been demonstrated by the migration of illegal crossings to more remote, less enforced areas. However, this migration has apparently not decreased the total number of illegal immigrants trying to cross. Recognizing that other factors may influence the rate of illegal immigration leads one to conclude that enforcement alone cannot control the rate of illegal immigration. A total deterrent effect could not be achieved unless the entire US-Mexico border was fenced and adequately manned, and even under those conditions it is certain that illegal crossing attempts would continue. Additionally, the cost to conduct such an enforcement operation could make it prohibitive and that cost could continue to escalate as illegal crossers adapt to the increased law enforcement. This raises a question of whether or not a different strategy and policy could create a more effective deterrent to illegal crossing attempts at less cost than manning and fencing the entire US-Mexico border.

US Policy

Prior to the 9/11 attacks the primary focus of border security was the prevention of illegal immigration, a difficult task considering the limited budget and resources plus the structurally ineffective organization of the enforcement agencies to share information and mutually support each other. The strategy to prevent illegal immigration was based upon a strategy of deterrence through enforcement. This strategy of deterrence is reflective in the laws passed in the last fifteen years, those that have failed to pass, and the sporadic increases in border security budgets, personnel, equipment and infrastructure.

After the 9/11 attacks the US continued with the same strategy of deterrence. However, the US also increased funding to more adequately support that strategy and reworded mission statements to reflect counter-terrorism as the primary mission. Additionally, the US restructured many of these enforcement organizations under DHS to facilitate the sharing of intelligence and synergy of effort.

Recognizing that resources are limited and the need to further mutually supportive combined action, the US government and supporting law enforcement agencies have adopted a risk management approach in determining resource employment. Unfortunately, based upon the GAO's findings and the current allocation of resources to the US-Mexico border versus the US-Canada border, DHS is still challenged in effectively determining the proper allocation of resources based upon risk (US Government Accountability Office 2007, 89-91).

Warranted or not, the US-Mexico border fence has come to symbolize the deterrence through enforcement strategy. Considering the location of the border fence and the limited deterrent effect it provides, one must question whether the fence provides the counter-terrorism deterrence effect intended. If the border fence is not intended to provide a substantial counter-terrorism effect then its cost also brings to question the proper allocation of resources.

As far as the alignment of strategic documents with addressing the terrorist threat is concerned, these documents appear to properly identify the threat and rank objectives accordingly. The 2007 NSHS does list preventing terrorist use of legitimate pathways into the US as its first method in denying terrorists entry to the homeland, and emphasizes the cooperation from bordering nations (National Strategy for Homeland

Security 2007, 18-19). Likewise, CBP lists prevention of terrorism between POEs second to prevention at POEs, and emphasizes partnerships with Canadian law enforcement and employing a balanced mix of trained personnel, equipment, and infrastructure (US Customs and Border Protection 2005, 14-16). USBP's objectives also support CBP's stated objectives. However, USBP emphasizes its mission on the US-Mexico border stating there is an ever present threat of terrorists using the same support structure used by illegal immigrants (US Border Patrol 2004, 5). The misalignment occurs in the methods to meet those objectives. While the documents state the priorities of effort, the results of investigations by the GAO demonstrate different actualities on the ground (US Government Accountability Office, Stana, 2008).

Using the old counter-illegal immigration strategy as the new counter-terrorism strategy, USBP has continued to deploy the majority of its personnel on the southern border instead of against the primary terrorist threat. Equating illegal immigration to terrorist infiltration has reinforced that focused deployment of personnel. While the USBP has increased the number of agents from 350 to 1,000 since 9/11, its personnel demand on the southern border has required its emphasis on technology to secure the northern border. Recognizing the personnel shortfall on the northern border the USBP has stated "the Border Patrol's ability to detect, respond to, and interdict illegal cross-border penetrations along the US-Canada border remains limited" (US Border Patrol 2004, 6)

Continuing to apply the old strategy for combating illegal immigration to the new counter-terrorism mission, the USBP has continued to use statistics on numbers of apprehensions of illegal immigrants as a measure of border security. The USBP contends

79

that lower apprehensions are due to the increased enforcement. This is exemplified in the Frontline articles written by Chief Aguilar (Aguilar 2008) and Linda Kane (Kane 2008) and in statements made by President Bush (Gonzalez 2007). However, the Chief Border Patrol Agent of the Blaine sector where Abu Mezer made his crossing stated that decreases in apprehensions in his sector were due to the detailing of manpower out of his sector to the southern border (US Department of Justice 1998). This suggests a problem with the USBP using an ineffective or misleading measure of performance (how well is the task being performed?) to measure the effectiveness (how well are we meeting the intended environmental impact?) of border security.

Recognizing that the CBP is only one agency among several that play a part in border security and that more than just the executive branch of the US government influence the direction of border security, achieving border security requires a whole of government approach. Chief Aguilar's comments on reducing illegal immigration to allow more agents to focus on "criminal activities and potential threats to our country" (Aguilar 2008, 10) allude to that whole of government approach. Legislation to curb the demand for cheap labor and facilitate Mexico's ability to employ its workforce may free more USBP agents to focus on their primary mission of counter-terrorism.

The application of the old counter-illegal immigration strategy as the new counter-terrorism strategy has maintained the focus of the USBP on the southern border instead of the threat. The focus on the southern border has also prevented the effective use of risk-based management to allocate resources according to the threat. This mis-application of strategy has also caused the continued use of the idea of "prevention through deterrence" for counter-terrorism strategy (US Border Patrol 2004, 8). To measure that deterrence the USBP uses numbers of apprehensions, which does not take into account the number of illegal immigrants that do get through, nor the fact that other factors may be affecting the number of apprehensions recorded. Without a good measure of effectiveness DHS cannot properly evaluate its strategy. Finally, the continued focus on the southern border has provided a means to provide, as Peter Andreas put it, "a perceptually appealing political salve for an extraordinarily difficult set of problems that have no easy short-term solutions" (Andreas 2000, 147-148). The US has attempted to eliminate or reduce illegal immigration at its southern border through infrastructure and enforcement, on the apparent assumption that such a reduction also deters or eliminates terrorist infiltration. It has also used questionable indicators of effectiveness to "prove" the success of such a strategy. In doing so, it has focused attention and resources on the obvious, physically tangible challenges, and away from the more difficult, less tangible challenges of economic motivation and a porous border adjoining a more "terrorist friendly" country to the north.

CHAPTER 5

CONCLUSIONS AND RECOMMENDATIONS

Conclusions

The US-Mexico border fence has only a limited deterrent effect against a terrorist, and that deterrent effect appears to be fleeting, even against illegal immigrants motivated solely by economic conditions and opportunities. Additionally, the fence does not have a significant defeat effect against a terrorist. As currently constructed and manned the fence has only turned illegal immigration to more remote, less enforced areas of the US-Mexico border without significantly reducing the numbers of illegal immigrants attempting to cross. However, that turning effect may dissipate as the illegal immigration support structure becomes more capable at subverting the increased enforcement. More importantly, as positioned, the border fence targets the bordering nation less likely to provide the conditions necessary to meet the terrorist's requirements for conducting a surreptitious border crossing.

An Al Qaeda or Al Qaeda inspired terrorist is the most likely and most capable terrorist to attempt a surreptitious crossing of the US land border. Based upon the Al Qaeda Manual and historical examples of terrorists gaining entrance into the US, a terrorist would require a Muslim population base, transportation, a hiding place, and possibly false documentation to carry out an operation. A Muslim population base is essential in providing the security and possible recruitment pool for this type of terrorist.

Apprehension data from the US-Mexico border and simulated border crossings indicate that a border fence would not deter terrorists attempting to cross the border; they would only be influenced in deciding where to cross. However, terrorists may regain the

82

ability to choose crossing sites on the US-Mexico border as the increasing and continued dependence of illegal immigrants on coyotes finances the improvement of coyotes' capabilities. The continued discovery of tunnels and other breaching methods along the border with the continued success of illegal immigrants to enter the US, even through areas of increased manning and surveillance, demonstrates the coyotes' increasing capabilities. Consequently, as currently constructed and planned the fence is not sufficient to deter or defeat a terrorist attempting to cross illegally. Additionally, when considering that a terrorist would most likely attempt his surreptitious crossing from Canada, it brings into question if the US-Mexico fence is necessary.

The fact remains that terrorists have historically gained access primarily by manipulating the immigration system (see Appendix A). The two times that a terrorist did attempt to enter the US via a land border occurred on the US-Canada border. Terrorists have not attempted to use the US-Mexico land border as a means to gain entrance into the US because the likelihood of success is greater by using either direct immigration into the US or indirect immigration through Canada. Coyotes may be able to fulfill a terrorist's requirements for transportation, a hiding place, and false documentation, but Mexico does not have the Muslim population to otherwise support an Al Qaeda or Al Qaeda inspired terrorist. Entry via Mexico consequently requires an additional assumption of risk on the part of the terrorist. The terrorist would have to depend upon non-Muslim facilitators, inhibiting his level of operational secrecy and security, and his ability to blend in with or recruit from the populace. Additionally, increased enforcement on the US-Mexico border further pushes him toward the already more appealing option of the US-Canada border. Traversing the border in the more

83

remote regions of the US-Mexico border and the increased law enforcement presence not only increases the likelihood of apprehension but also decreases the likelihood of surviving the crossing.

The major reason the US-Mexico border fence has a limited deterrence effect and no significant defeat effect is its positioning. The terrorist has a better likelihood for success at the US-Canada border. Canada's liberal immigration policies, provide not only ease in access to the North American continent, but also a large Muslim population for support or recruitment. This population has also demonstrated an ability to provide all of the terrorist's support requirements, and a pool for recruitment. Additionally, the conditions on the US-Canada border strengthen its appeal as a possible means of illegal entrance into the US. As demonstrated by the GAO investigation, lack of detection, lax enforcement, and easy access to road infrastructure provides the conditions for a higher likelihood of success (US Government Accountability Office 2007, 3-7). While the severe winter conditions along this border could provide a deterrent effect, they also provide offsetting opportunities. Severe winters freeze natural water barriers and degrade the operation of border security equipment, that equipment being the key to USBP's strategy to address the northern threat (US Border Patrol 2004, 6).

Recommendation

As stated by the GAO, "it remains vitally important for DHS to continue to develop and implement a risk-based framework to help target where and how the nation's resources should be invested to strengthen security" (US Government Accountability Office 2007, 93). Resources should be focused against the most likely terrorist threat to the US homeland, with priorities established accordingly. Based on the analysis of this study, those priorities for the security of the US land borders should be focused first on the US-Canada border and secondly on the US-Mexico border.

Unfortunately, the application and adaptation of the old USBP anti-illegal immigration strategy as the new counter-terrorism strategy has played a part in preventing the focusing of resources toward the terrorist threat. That is not to say that the USBP had any real choice in this matter. It is still a mission of the USBP to prevent and interdict illegal immigration across US borders. However, requiring USBP with its limited resources to conduct both the counter-terrorism mission along with an anti-illegal immigration mission has strained its ability to do both effectively. Freeing some of the manpower and technology required to perform the anti-illegal immigration mission would allow the refocusing of these resources toward the terrorist threat.

It is important to note that enforcement is only a part of the whole security strategy; consequently a "whole of government" approach is necessary. Enforcement alone cannot control the rate of illegal immigration; it can only provide the means to apprehend illegal immigrants. The US government must take steps to prevent attempts to cross illegally by focusing on reducing the motive to cross. Reducing attempts to cross illegally would not only free resources to focus on counter-terrorism operations, it would have a more direct counter-terrorism effect as well, by reducing the finances that enable the coyotes to continually increase the sophistication of their infiltration methods. These are the same infiltration methods that may provide the coyote with the means to transport a terrorist across the US-Mexico border.

This is not a recommendation that enforcement along the US-Mexico border should be decreased. A vigorous enforcement strategy on the US-Mexico border is a necessary part of the whole security strategy of the US homeland. The question remains as to what level of enforcement on the US land borders is necessary to meet the current threat, and if that threat can be more effectively reduced through steps other than enforcement.

Recommendations For Further Research

As was discussed in Chapter 4, the USBP has continued to use apprehension data as a measure of the effectiveness of its border security efforts. Consequently, the USBP has continually stated that reductions in apprehensions demonstrate the deterrence effect of increased enforcement. This use of the data is problematic not only because it does not take into account the numbers of illegal immigrants that are not apprehended, but it does not account for other factors that may influence the rate of illegal immigration. A research economist at Arizona State University, Dawn McLaren, has stated that there appears to be a correlation between the percentage growth in US GDP and numbers of apprehensions (Gonzalez 2007). However, Ms. McLaren's research did not provide any statistical proof of correlation. Additionally, other economic factors should be taken into consideration. As the apprehension data is from different sectors or stations, the state's economy corresponding to that sector's number of apprehensions may have been affected differently than is reflected by the nation's GDP growth. Percentage GDP growth also doesn't necessarily equate to employment opportunities. A study of economic indicators and other possible influencing factors could help the USBP to develop more appropriate methods for measuring the effectiveness of its border security efforts. Such a study could also provide further refinement for illegal immigration enforcement strategy through the development of more effective methods to identify and target these influencing factors.

Further study to define the terrorist threat in Canada and Mexico would prove beneficial to focusing counter-terrorism strategy. While the GAO did simulate the transport of radioactive material across the US land border, the availability of such material from those two nations was not addressed. Determination of the availability of such materials and the state of their security could further refine and strengthen binational security agreements, bringing the US, Canada, and Mexico another step forward in establishing a mutually supportive secure environment.

Summary

The US-Mexico border fence has only a limited deterrent effect against a terrorist attempting to enter the US surreptitiously from Mexico. So far, the fence has only turned illegal immigration to more remote, less enforced areas of the US-Mexico border. Its overall defeat or deterrent effect against a terrorist land crossing attempt is insignificant, primarily because of its positioning. The terrorist has a better likelihood for success at the US-Canada border. Canada's liberal immigration policies provide not only ease in access to the North American continent, but also a large Muslim population for support or recruitment. Resources should be focused against the most likely terrorist threat to the US homeland, with priorities established accordingly. USBP has assumed that illegal immigration equates to terrorist infiltration. Consequently, the application and adaptation of the old USBP anti-illegal immigration strategy as the new counter-terrorism strategy has played a major part in preventing the focusing of resources toward the primary terrorist threat. This has required USBP's limited resources to conduct both a counter-terrorism mission and an anti-illegal immigration mission, straining its ability to do both effectively. A vigorous enforcement strategy on the US-Mexico border is a necessary part of the whole security strategy of the US homeland, but enforcement must be combined with other steps to reduce illegal immigration. Enforcement alone cannot control the rate of illegal immigration. An over-emphasis on enforcement prevents the application of other complementary means to reduce the primary threat and the possible emergence of a new terrorist approach at the southern border.

GLOSSARY

coyotes. Individuals who smuggle illegal immigrants into the US. These individuals usually charge per individual and guide the illegal immigrant to a crossing site. In some cases the coyote may actually transport the illegal alien across the border. Coyotes conduct surveillance to determine the best times and locations for crossing the border and may also have inside information on USBP patrol routes and times.

border fence. a physical barrier constructed for the prevention or hindrance of a person's ability to traverse a boundary.

defeat. to render one unable or unwilling to pursue a course of action.

deter. to discourage one from a pursuing a course of action.

efficacy. capacity for producing a desired result or effect.

port of entry. an authorized location at which people or material may transverse a country's border for entry into that country.

SBInet. the US Customs and Border Protection program responsible for developing a comprehensive border protection system through a mix of security infrastructure, and surveillance and communication technologies.

Surreptitious border crossing. traversing another country's border at a location other than a port of entry without authorization from that country.

Terrorism. Premeditated, politically motivated violence perpetrated against noncombatant targets by subnational groups or clandestine agents (as defined by US law, Title 22 of the United States Code, Section 2656f(d)).

International Terrorism. Terrorism involving the territory or citizens of more than one country (as defined by US law, Title 22 of the United States Code, Section 2656f(d)).

Terrorist Group. Any group that practices, or has significant subgroups that practice international terrorism (as defined by US law, Title 22 of the United States Code, Section 2656f(d)).

virtual fence. a system for the detection of a traverse or attempted traverse of a boundary.

APPENDIX A

TERRORIST IMMIGRATION TABLE

The information in the following table has been assembled from data available in Michelle Malkin's book, Invasion. Malkin cited the Immigration and Naturalization Service, the Federal Bureau of Investigation, and the Center for Immigration Studies as her sources for the information (Malkin 2002, 239-242). The table provides a list of terrorists that had plotted or carried out terrorist attacks within the US. Information in this table was also verified with the 9/11 Commission Staff Monograph, 9/11 and Terrorist Travel (National Commission on Terrorist Attacks Upon the United States 2004). The author removed Lafi Khalil's name from the list in Malkin's book because he was acquitted of all charges in relation to the 1997 New York subway bombing plot.

Methods of Immigration

Name	Nationality	# of Entries	Terrorist Involvement	Remarks
Illegal Entrance				
Gazi Ibrahim Abu Mezer (Ghazi Ibrahim Abu Maizar)	Palestine	3	NY Subway Bombing Plot	2 attempts by foot, 3rd apprehended at bus station 25miles south of the Canadian border
Ahmed Ressam	Algeria	2	Millennium Bombing Plot	Transited LAX from Pakistan to Canada, 2nd entrance apprehended at Port Angeles POE
Abdelghani Meskini	Algeria	1	Millennium Bombing Plot	Ship stowaway landed in Boston
Abdel Hakim Tizegha	Algeria	1	Millennium Bombing Plot	Ship stowaway landed in Boston
Ahmad (Ahmed) Ajaj	Palestine	2	1993 WTC Bombing	Fraudulent passport, released after 6 mos.

Name	Nationality	# of Entries	Terrorist Involvement	Remarks
Illegal Entrance (cont.)				
Ramzi Yousef	Pakistan	1	1993 WTC Bombing	Fraudulent passport, claimed asylum and released
Remained Illegally After Legal Entrance				
Fadil Abdelghani	Sudan	1	NY Landmark Bombing Plot	Overstayed tourist visa, married American
Mohammed Abouhalima	Egypt	1	1993 WTC Bombing	Overstayed tourist visa, temp SAW[2] status later revoked
Mohammed Salameh	Jordan	1	1993 WTC Bombing	Overstayed tourist visa, denied SAW status, stayed anyway
Mahmud Abouhalima	Egypt	1	1993 WTC Bombing	Overstayed tourist visa, granted SAW amnesty
Nawaf al Hazmi	Saudi Arabia	1	9/11 Hijacker	Overstayed tourist visa, granted ID cards w/ expired visa
Satam Suqami	Saudi Arabia	1	9/11 Hijacker	Overstayed business visa
Hani Hanjour	Saudi Arabia	4	9/11 Hijacker	Overstayed student visa
Eyad Ismoil	Jordan	1	1993 WTC Bombing	Overstayed student visa
Zacarias Moussaoui	France	1	9/11 Conspirator	Overstayed visa waiver rules
Legally Immigrated				
Sheik Omar Abdel Rahman	Egypt	>3	NY Landmark Bombing Plot	Numerous tourist visas despite on watch list, legal permanent resident status revoked, applied for asylum
Saeed (Saaed) al Ghamdi	Saudi Arabia	1	9/11 Hijacker	Tourist visa

[2] Seasonal Agricultural Worker (SAW) program, a provision of the Immigration Reform and Control Act of 1986 through which agricultural workers could apply for legal resident status

Name	Nationality	# of Entries	Terrorist Involvement	Remarks
Legally Immigrated (cont.)				
Ziad Jarrah	Saudi Arabia	7	9/11 Hijacker	Did not overstay tourist visa, but failed to change to student while attending flight school
Mohammed Atta	Egypt	3	9/11 Hijacker	Tourist visa, allowed in despite previous overstay
Marwan Al Shehhi	United Arab Emirates	3	9/11 Hijacker	Tourist visa, allowed in despite previous overstay
Ahmed al Ghamdi	Saudi Arabia	1	9/11 Hijacker	Tourist visa
Waleed al Shehri	Saudi Arabia	1	9/11 Hijacker	Tourist visa
Wail al Shehri	Saudi Arabia	1	9/11 Hijacker	Tourist visa
Abdul Aziz al Omari (Abdulaziz Alomari)	Saudi Arabia	1	9/11 Hijacker	Tourist visa
Fayez (Ahmed) Banihammad	Saudi Arabia	1	9/11 Hijacker	Tourist visa
Mohand al Shehri	Saudi Arabia	1	9/11 Hijacker	Tourist visa
Hamza (Hazma) al Ghamdi	Saudi Arabia	1	9/11 Hijacker	Tourist visa
Majed Moqed	Saudi Arabia	1	9/11 Hijacker	Tourist visa
Salem al Hazmi	Saudi Arabia	1	9/11 Hijacker	Tourist visa
Ahmed al Haznawi	Saudi Arabia	1	9/11 Hijacker	Tourist visa
Ahmad (Ahmed) Alnami	Saudi Arabia	1	9/11 Hijacker	Tourist visa
Khalid al Mihdhar (Almidhdhar)	Saudi Arabia	1	9/11 Hijacker	Business visa
El Sayyid Nosair	Egypt	1	NY Landmark Bombing Plot	Tourist visa, married American
Amir Abdelgani	Sudan	1	NY Landmark Bombing Plot	Tourist visa, married American
Wadih el Hage	Lebanon	1	US Embassy Bombings in Africa	Student visa, married American

Name	Nationality	# of Entries	Terrorist Involvement	Remarks
Legally Immigrated (cont.)				
Khalid Abu al Dahab	Egypt	1	US Embassy Bombings in Africa	Student visa, married American
Ali Mohammed	Egypt		US Embassy Bombings in Africa	Married American, became naturalized citizen
Siddig Ibrahim Siddig Ali	Sudan		NY Landmark Bombing Plot	Married American, became legal resident
Tarig Elhassan	Sudan		NY Landmark Bombing Plot	Married American, became legal resident
Abdo Mohammed Haggag	Egypt		NY Landmark Bombing Plot	Married American, became legal resident
Fares Khallafalla	Sudan		NY Landmark Bombing Plot	Married American, became legal resident
Matarawy Mohammed Said Saleh	Egypt		NY Landmark Bombing Plot	Married American, became legal resident
Mohammed Saleh	Palestine		NY Landmark Bombing Plot	Married American, became legal resident
Essam al Ridi	Egypt	1	US Embassy Bombings in Africa	Student, became naturalized citizen
Nidal Ayyad	Kuwait	1	1993 WTC Bombing	Joined Father in US, became naturalized citizen
Ibrahim Ilgabrowny (Elgabrowny)	Egypt		NY Landmark Bombing Plot	Legal Permanent Resident
Richard Reid	United Kingdom	N/A	2001 Shoe Bomber Attempt	Apprehended in flight to US from Paris

Source: Author Created, Information from Malkin, Michelle. 2002. *Invasion.* and National Commission on Terrorist Attacks Upon the United States. 2004. *9/11 and Terrorist Travel.*

REFERENCE LIST

Aguilar, David V. 2008. "Protecting the Southern Border." *Frontline,* Spring. http://www.cbp.gov/linkhandler/cgov/newsroom/publications/frontline_magazine/ frontline.ctt/frontline.pdf (accessed October 16, 2008).

Al Qaeda Manual. n.d. Seized in 2000. The Smoking Gun. http://www.thesmokinggun. com/archive/jihadmanual.html (accessed September 12, 2008).

Andreas, Peter. 2000. *Border Games: Policing the U.S.-Mexico Divide.* Ithaca: Cornell University Press.

Anti-Defamation League. 2004. *Terrorism Update. Canada and Terrorism. Anti-Defamation League,* January. http://www.adl.org/terror/tu/tu_0401_canada.asp (accessed October 8, 2008).

Associated Press. 2006. "Canada nabs 17 terror suspects in Toronto." *USA Today,* June 4, http://www.usatoday.com/news/world/2006-06-03-toronto-terror-suspects_x.htm (accessed November 7, 2008).

Associated Press. 2006. "Calderon Likens Fence to Berlin Wall." *CBS News,* October 26, http://www.cbsnews.com/stories/2006/10/26/world/main2130155.shtml (accessed October 10, 2008).

BBC News. 2004. "Mexico to extradite Eta suspects." *BBC News Online,* July 31, http://news.bbc.co.uk/nolpda/ukfs_news/hi/newsid_3941000/3941703.stm (accessed October 8, 2008).

Bernton, Hal, Mike Carter, David Heath, and James Neff. 2002. "The Terrorist Within, Chapter 1: The Past as Prologue." *Seattle Times.* June 23. http://community. seattletimes.nwsource.com/archive/?date=20020623&slug=1ressam23 (accessed November 5, 2008).

Bernton, Hal, Mike Carter, David Heath, and James Neff. 2002. "The Terrorist Within, Chapter 2: The Fountainhead." *Seattle Times.* June 23. http://community. seattletimes.nwsource.com/archive/?date=20020623&slug=2ressam230 (accessed November 5, 2008).

Bernton, Hal, Mike Carter, David Heath, and James Neff. 2002. "The Terrorist Within, Chapter 3: Leaving home." *Seattle Times.* June 23. http://community.seattletimes. nwsource.com/archive/?date=20020623&slug=3ressam23 (accessed November 5, 2008).

Bernton, Hal, Mike Carter, David Heath, and James Neff. 2002. "The Terrorist Within, Chapter 4: Sneaking in." *Seattle Times.* June 24. http://community.seattletimes. nwsource.com/archive/?date=20020624&slug=4ressam24 (accessed November 5, 2008).

Bernton, Hal, Mike Carter, David Heath, and James Neff. 2002. "The Terrorist Within, Chapter 5: The Terrorist Tracker." *Seattle Times.* June 25. http://community. seattletimes.nwsource.com/archive/?date=20020625&slug=5ressam25 (accessed November 5, 2008).

Bernton, Hal, Mike Carter, David Heath, and James Neff. 2002. "The Terrorist Within, Chapter 6: It Takes a Thief." *Seattle Times.* June 26. http://community.seattletimes. nwsource.com/archive/?date=20020626&slug=6ressam26 (accessed November 5, 2008).

Bernton, Hal, Mike Carter, David Heath, and James Neff. 2002. "The Terrorist Within, Chapter 7: Joining Jihad." *Seattle Times.* June 27. http://community.seattletimes. nwsource.com/archive/?date=20020627&slug=7ressam27 (accessed November 5, 2008).

Bernton, Hal, Mike Carter, David Heath, and James Neff. 2002. "The Terrorist Within, Chapter 8: Going to Camp." *Seattle Times.* June 28. http://community. seattletimes.nwsource.com/archive/?date=20020628&slug=8ressam28 (accessed November 5, 2008).

Bernton, Hal, Mike Carter, David Heath, and James Neff. 2002. "The Terrorist Within, Chapter 9: 'A Bunch of Guys'." *Seattle Times.* June 29. http://community. seattletimes.nwsource.com/archive/?date=20020629&slug=9ressam29 (accessed November 5, 2008).

Bernton, Hal, Mike Carter, David Heath, and James Neff. 2002. "The Terrorist Within, Chapter 10: The Mission." *Seattle Times.* June 30. http://community.seattletimes. nwsource.com/archive/?date=20020630&slug=10ressam30 (accessed November 5, 2008).

Bernton, Hal, Mike Carter, David Heath, and James Neff. 2002. "The Terrorist Within, Chapter 11: The Ticking Bomb." *Seattle Times.* July 1. http://community. seattletimes.nwsource.com/archive/?date=20020701&slug=11ressam01 (accessed November 5, 2008).

Bernton, Hal, Mike Carter, David Heath, and James Neff. 2002. "The Terrorist Within, Chapter 12: The Crossing." *Seattle Times.* July 2. http://community.seattletimes. nwsource.com/archive/?date=20020702&slug=12ressam02 (accessed November 5, 2008).

Bernton, Hal, Mike Carter, David Heath, and James Neff. 2002. "The Terrorist Within, Chapter 13: On the Case." *Seattle Times.* July 3. http://community.seattletimes. nwsource.com/archive/?date=20020703&slug=13ressam03 (accessed November 5, 2008).

Bernton, Hal, Mike Carter, David Heath, and James Neff. 2002. "The Terrorist Within, Chapter 14: The Warning." *Seattle Times.* July 4. http://community.seattletimes. nwsource.com/archive/?date=20020704&slug=14ressam04 (accessed November 5, 2008).

Bernton, Hal, Mike Carter, David Heath, and James Neff. 2002. "The Terrorist Within, Chapter 15: Puzzle Pieces." *Seattle Times.* July 5. http://community.seattletimes. nwsource.com/archive/?date=20020705&slug=15ressam05 (accessed November 5, 2008).

Bernton, Hal, Mike Carter, David Heath, and James Neff. 2002. "The Terrorist Within, Chapter 16: The Reckoning." *Seattle Times.* July 6. http://community.seattletimes. nwsource.com/archive/?date=20020706&slug=16ressam06 (accessed November 5, 2008).

Bernton, Hal, Mike Carter, David Heath, and James Neff. 2002. "The Terrorist Within, Chapter 17: Nine-Eleven." *Seattle Times.* July 7. http://community.seattletimes. nwsource.com/archive/?date=20020707&slug=17ressam07 (accessed November 5, 2008).

Border Security Conference. 2008. *A Binational Strategy for Border Protection and Effective Commerce.* Conference held at The University of Texas at El Paso. August 11-12.

Buchanan, Patrick J. 2006. *State of Emergency.* New York: St. Martin's Press.

Carl, Traci. 2008. "Mexico Looks for Tall, Repentant Grenade-Thrower." *Associated Press,* September 17. http://abcnews.go.com/International/wireStory?id=5820203 (accessed October 7, 2008).

Canada in the Making. Specific Events & Topics, Immigration Acts 1866-2001. http://www.canadiana.org/citm/specifique/immigration_e.html (accessed November 1-6, 2008).

Census of Canada. 2001.Religions in Canada: Provincial and territorial highlights, 2001. http://www12.statcan.ca/english/census01/Products/Analytic/companion/rel/provs .cfm (accessed November 6, 2008).

CIA. The World Factbook. Canada. http://www.cia.gov/library/publications/the-world-factbook/geos/ca.html (accessed October 7, 2008).

CIA. The World Factbook. Mexico. http://www.cia.gov/library/publications/the-world-factbook/geos/mx.html (accessed October 7, 2008).

Consolidated Appropriations Act of 2008. Public Law 110-161. 110th Cong., 1st sess. January 4. http://thomas.loc.gov/cgi-bin/query/z?c110:H.R.2764.enr: (accessed April 17, 2008).

Coyle, Harold, and Barret Tillman. 2007. *Pandora's Legion: Strategic Solutions INC.* New York: Forge.

Cragin, Kim, and Sara A. Daly. 2004. *The Dynamic Terrorist Threat: An Assessment of Group Motivations and Capabilities in a Changing World.* Santa Monica: Rand Corporation.

Egan, Timothy. 1997. "Easy Illegal U.S. Entry in Northwest." *The New York Times,* August 7. http://query.nytimes.com/gst/fullpage.html?res=9B06EED9173CF93 4A3575BC0A961958260&scp=1&sq=Easy+Illegal+U.S.+Entry+in+Northwest& st=nyt (accessed May 3, 2008).

Feldner, Yotam. 2004. "The Saudi Separation Fence." *The Middle East Media Research Institute*, series no. 162, February 13.

FOX News. 2005. "Illegal Alien Influx May Compromise Security." March 16. http://www.foxnews.com/story/0,2933,150520,00.html (accessed October 2, 2008).

Garcia, Miguel. 2008. "Grenade attacks kill 8 on Mexico's national day." *International Herald Tribune, Reuters,* September 16. http://www.iht.com/articles/reuters/ 2008/09/16/america/OUKWD-UK-MEXICO-BLASTS.php (accessed October 7, 2008).

Garvin, Natascha. 2005. "Conversion & Conflict: Muslims in Mexico." *ISIM Review,* Spring. http://www.isim.nl/files/Review_15/Review_15-18.pdf (accessed October 7, 2008).

Gilbert, James. 2008. "Possible tunnel on border brings Yuma-area arrest." *Yuma Sun,* November 10. http://www.azstarnet.com/allheadlines/266502 (accessed November 11, 2008).

Glüsing, Jens. 2005. "Islam is Gaining a Foothold in Chiapas." *Spiegel Online International,* May 28. http://www.spiegel.de/international/spiegel/0,1518, 358223,00.html (accessed October 7, 2008).

Gonzalez, Daniel. 2007. "Drop in illegal crossings tied to slow economy, not troops, experts say." *Arizona Republic,* May 9. http://www.usatoday.com/news/nation/ 2007-05-09-illegal-crossings_N.htm (accessed November 9, 2008).

Hanson, Gordon H. 2007. "The Economic Logic of Illegal Immigration." *Council On Foreign Relations,* CSR no. 26 (April). United States: Council On Foreign Relations. http://www.cfr.org/content/publications/attachments/Immigration CSR26.pdf (accessed October 8, 2008).

Hendricks, Tyche. 2006. "Border security or boondoggle? A plan for 700 miles of Mexican border walls heads for Senate." *The San Francisco Chronicle*, February 26. http://www.sfgate.com/cgi-bin/article.cgi?file=/c/a/2006/02/26/ MNGHIHDUQF1.DTL (accessed March 26, 2008).

Hendricks, Tyche. 2007. "Study: Price for border fence up to $49 billion." *The San Francisco Chronicle*, January 8. http://www.sfgate.com/cgi-bin/article.cgi?f= /c/a/2007/01/08/BAG6RNEJJG1.DTL (accessed March 26, 2008).

Kane, Linda. 2008. "Along The Northern Border." *Frontline,* Spring. http://www.cbp.gov/linkhandler/cgov/newsroom/publications/frontline_magazine/ frontline.ctt/frontline.pdf (accessed October 16, 2008).

Jacobs, Karen. 2006. "Immigration rallies sweep through U.S. cities." *Reuters,* April 11. http://thestaronline.com/news/story.asp?file=/2006/4/11/worldupdates/2006-04-11T023348Z_01_NOOTR_RTRJONC_0_-244349-1&sec=Worldupdates (accessed October 3, 2008).

Lacey, Marc. 2008. "Grenade Attack in Mexico Breaks From Deadly Script." *New York Times,* September 25. http://www.nytimes.com/2008/09/25/world/americas/25 mexico.html?_r=1&fta=y (accessed October 7, 2008).

Lange, Jason. 2008. "Colombia asks Mexico to probe ties with rebels." *Reuters.com,* March 14. http://www.reuters.com/article/email/idUSN1445284720080315? sp=true (accessed October 8, 2008).

Library of Congress. Federal Research Division. 2003. *Organized Crime and Terrorist Activity in Mexico, 1999-2002*, (February). by Ramón Miró and Glen E. Curtis. http://www.loc.gov/rr/frd/pdf-files/OrgCrime_Mexico.pdf (accessed October 8, 2008).

Library of Congress. Congressional Research Service. 2005. *Border Security: The Role of the US Border Patrol,* no. RL32562 (May 10). by Blas Nuñez-Neto. Report for Congress.

Library of Congress. Congressional Research Service. 2007. *Border Security: the San Diego Fence,* no. RS22026 (May 23). by Blas Nuñez-Neto. Report for Congress.

Library of Congress. Congressional Research Service. 2008. *Border Security: Barriers Along the US International Border,* no. RL33659 (May 13). by Blas Nuñez-Neto. Report for Congress.

Malkin, Michelle. 2002. *Invasion.* Washington, D.C.: Regnery Publishing, Inc..

Manheim, Jarol B., Richard C. Rich, Lars Willnat, and Craig Leonard Brians. 2008. *Empirical Political Analysis: Quantitative and Qualitative Research Methods.* 7th edition. New York: Pearson Education, Inc..

Marosi, Richard. 2008. "Mexico border tunnel suspects charged." *Los Angeles Times,* September 17. http://articles.latimes.com/2008/sep/17/world/fg-tunnel17 (accessed October 7, 2008).

Mexican Trucker Online blog. 2008. *The Truth behind the Narco Wars in Cd. Juarez,* entry posted June 2. http://mexicotrucker.com/2008/06/02/the-truth-behind-the-narco-wars-in-cd-juarez/ (accessed October 3, 2008).

Mikkelsen, Randall. 2008. "U.S. official defends 'virtual' border barrier." *Reuters.com,* March 5. http://www.reuters.com/article/domesticNews/id USN0536848220080305 (accessed April 24, 2008).

Miles, Matthew B., and A. Michael Huberman. 1984. *Qualitative Data Analysis: A Sourcebook of New Methods.* Newbury Park: Sage Publications, Inc..

National Commission on Terrorist Attacks Upon the United States. 2004. *9/11 and Terrorist Travel,* Staff Report of the National Commission on Terrorist Attacks Upon the United States (September 21). by Thomas R. Eldridge, Susan Ginsburg, Walter T. Hempel II, Janice L. Kephart, and Kelly Moore. http://www.9-11commission.gov/staff_statements/911_TerrTrav_Monograph.pdf (accessed November 1, 2008).

Patton, Michael Quinn. 1990. *Qualitative Evaluation and Research Methods.* 2nd edition. Newbury Park: Sage Publications, Inc.

Payan, Tony. 2006. *The Three U.S.-Mexico Border Wars: Drugs, Immigration, and Homeland Security.* Connecticut: Praeger Security International.

Pike, John. "US-Mexico Border Fence/Great Wall of Mexico." *GlobalSecurity.org,* http://www.globalsecurity.org/security/systems/mexico-wall.htm.

Rasmussen Reports. 2007. "Why the Senate Immigration Bill Failed." *Rasmussen Reports,* June 8. http://www.rasmussenreports.com/public_content/politics/ current_events/immigration/why_the_senate_immigration_bill_failed (accessed October 3, 2008).

Rodriguez, Olga R. 2008. "2 suspects describe grenade attacks in Mexico." *Associated Press,* September 27. http://www.boston.com/news/world/latinamerica/articles/ 2008/09/27/mexico_arrests_3_suspects_in_grenade_attack/ (accessed October 7, 2008).

Secure Fence Act of 2006. Public law 109-367. 109th Cong., 2d sess. January 3.
 http://frwebgate.access.gpo.gov/cgi-bin/getdoc.cgi?dbname=109_cong_bills
 &docid=f:h6061enr.txt.pdf (accessed April 17, 2008)

Smick, Elisabeth. 2006. "Backgrounder. Canada's Immigration Policy." *Council on
 Foreign Relations,* July 6. http://www.cfr.org/publication/11047/#1 (accessed
 October 3, 2008).

Tancredo, Tom. 2006. *Mortal Danger: The Battle for America's Border and Security.*
 Nashville: Cumberland House Publishing, Inc..

US Border Patrol. 2004. *National Border Patrol Strategy* (September), Prepared by The
 Office of Border Patrol and The Office of Policy and Planning, Washington DC:
 US Customs & Border Protection.

US Congress. Congressional Budget Office. 2006. *Immigration Policy in the United
 States,* (February). http://www.cbo.gov/ftpdocs/70xx/doc7051/02-28-
 Immigration.pdf (accessed October 16, 2008).

US Congress. House. 2005. *Border Protection, Antiterrorism, and Illegal Immigration
 Control Act of 2005.* HR 4437. 109th Cong., 1st sess., (December 16).
 http://thomas.loc.gov/cgi-bin/bdquery/z?d109:h.r.04437: (accessed April 20,
 2008).

US Congress. Senate. 2006. *Comprehensive Immigration Reform Act of 2006.* S 2611.
 109th Cong., 2nd sess., (May 25). http://thomas.loc.gov/cgi-bin/query/z?
 c109:S.2611: (accessed April 20, 2008).

US Customs and Border Protection. 2005. *Protecting America: US Customs and Border
 Protection 2005-2010 Strategic Plan,* (May), Prepared by The Office of Policy
 and Planning, Washington DC: US Customs & Border Protection.

US Department of Homeland Security.2002. *National Strategy for Homeland Security,*
 (July), Prepared by Homeland Security Council, Washington, DC: Government
 Printing Office.

US Department of Homeland Security. 2007. *National Strategy for Homeland Security,*
 (October), Prepared by Homeland Security Council, Washington, DC:
 Government Printing Office.

US Department of Justice. Office of the Inspector General. 1998. *Bombs in Brooklyn:
 How the Two Illegal Aliens Arrested for Plotting to Bomb the New York Subway
 Entered and Remained in the United States,* (March). http://fas.org/irp/agency/
 doj/oig/brookb/brbrtoc.htm (accessed June 10, 2008).

US Government Accountability Office. 2007. *Homeland Security: Progress Has Been Made to Address the Vulnerabilities Exposed by 9/11, but Continued Federal Action Is Needed to Further Mitigate Security Risks*, no. GAO-07-375 (January), Report to Congressional Requesters, House of Representatives.

US Government Accountability Office. 2007. *Border Security: Security Vulnerabilities at Unmanned and Unmonitored US Border Locations*, no. GAO-07-884T (September 27), Testimony before the Committee on Finance, US Senate. Statement of Gregory D. Kutz.

US Government Accountability Office. 2007. *Secure Border Initiative: Observations on Selected Aspects of SBInet Program Implementation*, no. GAO-08-131T (October 24), Testimony before the Subcommittees on Management, Investigations, and Oversight, and Border, Maritime and Global Counterterrorism, Committee on Homeland Security, House of Representatives. Statement of Richard M. Stana.

US Government Accountability Office. 2008. *Homeland Security: DHS Has Taken Actions to Strengthen Border Security Programs and Operations, but Challenges Remain*, no. GAO-08-542T (March 6), Testimony before the Subcommittee on Homeland Security, Committee on Appropriations, House of Representatives. Statement of Richard M. Stana.

US National Intelligence Council. 2007. *National Intelligence Estimate, The Terrorist Threat to the US Homeland,* (October), Prepared by National Intelligence Council, Washington, DC: Government Printing Office. http://dni.gov/press_releases/20070717_release.pdf (accessed October 5, 2008).

US National Security Council. 2006. *National Strategy for Combating Terrorism,* (September), Prepared by the National Security Council, Washington, DC: Government Printing Office. http://www.whitehouse.gov/nsc/nsct/2006/ (accessed October 5, 2008).

Waller, J. Michael. 2006. "Mexico's Glass House." *Center for Security Policy*, April 6. http://www.c4ads.org/files/waller_csp_apr2006_mexico.pdf (accessed October 3, 2008).

Waller, J. Michael. 2006. "Mexico's Immigration Law: Let's Try it Here at Home." *Citizens For a Constitutional Republic,* May 8. http://www.citizensfora constitutionalrepublic.com/waller5-8-06.html (accessed October 3, 2008).

Wilkinson, Tracy. 2008. "Morelia suspect tells of holding grenade." *Los Angeles Times,* September 28. http://www.latimes.com/news/nationworld/world/la-fg-mexico28-2008sep28,0,1254529.story (accessed October 7, 2008).

Zambellis, Chris. 2006. "Islamic Radicalism in Mexico: The Threat from South of the Border." *The Jamestown Foundation. Terrorism Monitor* Volume 4, Issue 11 (June 2). http://www.jamestown.org/terrorism/news/article.php?articleid= 2370015 (accessed October 7, 2008).